Helpings for the Heart

GEORGE E. VANDEMAN

Pacific Press® Publishing Association
Nampa, Idaho
Oshawa, Ontario, Canada
www.pacificpress.com

Cover design by Mark Bond
Cover design resources from Getty Images, Inc.
Inside design by Steve Lanto

Unless otherwise credited, Scripture quotations are from the Holy Bible,
New King James Version, copyright © 1979, 1980, 1982 by Thomas Nelson,
Inc., Publishers. Used by permission.

Additional copies of this book are available by calling toll-free 1-800-765-6955
or online at http://www.adventistbookcenter.com.

Library of Congress Cataloging-in-Publication Data

Vandeman, George E.
Helpings for the Heart : *It Is Written* Founder George Vandeman's
Favorite Stories / by George E. Vandeman.
      p. cm.
ISBN 13: 978-0-8163-2272-5
ISBN 10: 0-8163-2272-4
1. Christian life. 2. Homiletical illustrations. I. Title.
BV4515.3.V36 2008
242—dc22
                                          2008002502

08 09 10 11 12 • 5 4 3 2 1

Contents

Helpings for the Heart

*I*ntroduction

My mother was the best cook in the world. Maybe we all say that about our mothers, but I *know* mine was the very best. She was particularly known for all varieties of homemade soups—from lentil to split pea to navy bean to creamy potato to savory vegetable. Every Friday afternoon the aromatic blend of legumes, vegetables, and seasonings could be found simmering in a large pot on the stove. Supper on Friday night consisted of endless helpings of soup and homemade bread. Homemade soup was always my father's favorite food, and it's still my favorite comfort food, fifty-plus years later. Not only was Mom's cooking nourishing and just downright tasty, it fed something more than our physical appetites. Her soup was a symbol of togetherness, comfort, belonging, and ultimately, love.

My father was not a cook. Later in life, he bought a bread machine and tried his hand at homemade bread. His bread was pretty good. But while Mom was the homemaker and cook, Dad was the preacher. George Vandeman was a television evangelist and founded the *It Is Written* ministry in 1956—the year I was born. His ministry spanned six decades. For two thousand consecutive Sundays Dad could be seen on the *It Is Written* telecast. He was an author, a teacher, a preacher, and a wonderful storyteller. While Mom's food fed our physical hunger, Dad's inspiring stories and sermon illustrations fed our hearts and souls.

I was fortunate to belong to a family that was uniquely Seventh-day Adventist. Not only did I grow up an Adventist—I grew up a Vandeman. It didn't get much more *Adventist* than that! For me, Adventism was, and still is, the framework of my faith. It provides a community of support and a belief system that continues to serve me well to this day. All of us, whatever our faith background, need giant helpings of healing, encouragement, and inspiration to feed our hearts and to help us grow and be spiritually healthy on our journeys. That's what I hope this collection of my father's most inspiring stories and sermon illustrations does for you.

Just as my mother's homemade soups were a blend of vegetables and seasonings, so this collection of *Helpings for the Heart* is a blend of my dad's most powerful stories as well as some short, sweet vignettes. And all of these stories are *uniquely Adventist.* For me, to be *uniquely Adventist* means that I keep my faith while being open, honest, complicated at times, compassionate, searching, full of joy, able to cry, and confident of the amazing grace of Jesus Christ. It means I hold to my faith no matter what. And most importantly, it means I need to love others just as Christ loved me. Do I live up to all that? Not by a long shot. But when we are *uniquely Adventist,* we are surrounded by people who lift us up when we fall, who dust us off and point us to the only perfect One. I like that about us. So did my father.

I'll never be the cook by mother was or the storyteller my dad was, but I'd like to invite you over for Friday night supper to share a helping or two of soup and to talk about what God continues to do in our lives— yours and mine. Whether you are a long time Adventist like me or a young or old Adventist or one who left long ago and wonders if there's a way back; whether you are unsure of your own faith and want another *helping for your heart.* . . . remember this: You are family, the table is set, and soup's on.

Enjoy!

Connie Vandeman Jeffery
January 2008

$\mathscr{S}$andy and the Angel

Nine-year-old Tommy, wet and bedraggled in his angel costume and yellow wig, sat in a tree not far from the bridge that might collapse at any moment. He had been at the school, practicing for the Easter pageant. He hadn't wanted to be in the pageant. After all, what nine-year-old boy wants to be cast as an angel with wings and yellow curls? But his mother had insisted.

On the way home from rehearsal, a violent storm had come up. Tommy knew that the bridge could not be trusted in a storm. It was one that a group of neighbors had built to save going ten miles around the lake. His father had told him in a situation like this just to climb a tree and wait for Dad to come after him. So, Tommy was waiting.

Through the dense fog he saw lights approaching. As the car came into view, he saw that it was old Sandy McPherson. None of the neighbors had ever seen Sandy sober. If he had been drinking now, and he almost certainly had, he might not use good judgment. He might drive onto the precarious bridge.

So, Tommy called out as loud as he could, "Sandy, don't take the bridge! Go around the lake!"

Tommy started to climb down from the tree, for surely Sandy would take him home. But Sandy took off as if he had seen a ghost!

A few minutes later, Tommy's father, on his way to pick up his son, met Sandy on the road. Sandy got out of his car—pale, his lips quivering, his hands shaking. For the first time in anyone's memory, he was cold sober. "You won't believe me," he gasped, "but I just saw a vision! God hasn't forgotten me! The good God—He hasn't forgotten me!"

Tommy's father tried to calm him. "Take a deep breath and tell me slowly. You must get ahold of yourself."

"Well, I'd had a few drops of whiskey, to keep the chill off, you understand. It was getting dark, and the visibility was zero. I was about to turn onto the bridge when I heard a voice say, 'Sandy, don't take the bridge! Go around the lake!'

"I looked up," Sandy continued, still out of breath, "and there, floating between the trees, was an angel! Dressed in white, he was, with wings on his shoulders and yellow curls on his head!"

"What did you do?"

"I threw my bottle out of the car with all my force. If the good God thinks enough of old Sandy McPherson to send an angel to warn him, I won't be a party to destroying myself!"

And Sandy was never known to take another drink as long as he lived!

Fearfully and Wonderfully Made

A small boy was asked to write an essay about anatomy. This is what he wrote:

Your head is kind of round and hard, and your brains are in it, and your hair is on it. Your face is in front of your head, where you eat. Your neck is what keeps your head, off your shoulders, which are sort of shelves where you hook your overall's suspenders.

Your arms you got to have to pitch baseballs with and so you can reach the biscuits. Your fingers stick out of your hand so you can scratch, throw a curveball, and add arithmetic. Your legs is what you got to have to get to first base, your feet is what you run on, and your toes are what gets stubbed.

And that's all there is of you except what's inside, and I ain't seen that!

There's been some disagreement about what's inside us and how we are put together. Are we just a body with a brain and nothing else? Is there a spiritual component that is as much "us" as is our body and our mind?

Jesus knew how human beings were made. He knew we were made in one piece—body, mind, and spirit. And so He healed the bodies of men and women so that they would have clear minds to accept Him and to follow Him with all their hearts and with all their minds.

An Honest Farmer

A city attorney wanted to buy a horse. So, he went out into the country and found a fine-looking horse he wanted to purchase. The farmer agreed to sell the horse if the city man could catch him.

That didn't seem too unreasonable. The lawyer took his two sons out into the pasture. But it took them three hours to corral the horse and put a bridle on him.

And then the farmer, being a meticulously honest man, said to the prospective buyer, "There are two things I have to tell you about this horse before I take your money. In the first place, he is awful hard to catch."

Well, the lawyer knew that.

"The second thing," said the farmer, "is this. He's not worth a hill of beans when you've caught him."

We're all selling ourselves to other people all the time—or trying to. And we're very particular about the display counter. We want to look right and sound right and seem right. And if we're a little hard to catch— well, that's all right too.

But if we were as honest as that farmer, would we have to warn any prospective "buyer" that we aren't worth very much once we've been caught? The truth is that we go to great lengths to hide our flaws. We don't want anyone to guess that we have a temper that is apt to explode at any moment if someone says the wrong thing. We don't want anyone to know that we aren't as calm and composed and gracious on the inside as we are on the outside.

A lot of advice is making the rounds today. "Just be yourself. Act natural." But is that a good idea? How do we act when we act natural? What are we like when we let go the restraints?

A person may go to church every week and carry a Bible. But someone has reminded us that a chimpanzee can be trained to carry a Bible.

Calling Sin by Its Right Name

During the energy crisis of 1973, when drivers were lined up at gas stations, trying to get enough gas to keep their cars running, someone got the idea to ask a number of school children for ideas about how to solve the energy problem. A newspaper published the kids' ideas. Here are some of the more creative suggestions:

"Help out around filling stations so the owners will have more time to go out and drill for oil."

"Everyone who visits a foreign country that has a lot of oil should bring back a quart with them."

"Keep a dog in the car that is trained to bark if the car goes faster than fifty miles an hour."

But the best suggestion came from one little girl. "Find out if there is another name for oil," she said, "and look for it under that name."

That's what a lot of us have been doing with sin. We've been trying to find other names for it and trying to deal with it under those names. We like to think of our sins as simply innocent mistakes or errors in judgment or the result of a deficiency in our personality. We like to call sin anything but its right name. We will never make progress in the Christian life until we come to terms with our own sinful condition and learn to call sin by its right name.

Jesus said He came to call sinners to repentance. He called sin by its right name. He also forgave sins. He said, "Son, your sins are forgiven."

He said, "Go, and sin no more" (see Luke 5:20; John 8:11).

It's Not Easy to Let Go!

A man was chasing a rabbit through the woods. He was almost on the rabbit, the story goes, when suddenly they came to the edge of a cliff. The rabbit, of course, had the advantage. It was small and agile and able to make a quick turn and avoid going over the precipice. But the man couldn't turn as quickly, and went over.

As he was falling, he was able to reach out and grab a small bush growing out of the side of the cliff. It stopped his fall and held his weight. Now the man was hanging on for dear life.

He began to scream for help. He shouted, "Can anyone hear me?" There was no answer. He yelled again, louder this time, "Is anyone up there?"

Finally he heard a deep voice from somewhere up above, "To whom do you wish to speak?"

And the man, desperately clinging to the bush, managed to shout, "Anyone who will help me."

Then, according to the story, the voice from above asked, "Do you have faith?"

And the man replied, "Yes." He hoped it was true.

"All right," the voice continued, "if you have faith, let go of that bush!"

The man hesitated. He looked down. It was a *long* way down! All that stood between him and certain death, it seemed, was that little bush. Finally, after a long silence, the man shouted, "Is there anyone *else* up there?"

We think we have faith in God. We talk about it. We boast about it. And we get along fine—as long as our faith isn't challenged. But when it is—when we get into a tight spot where we have to throw our full weight on our faith, where we have to demonstrate it or deny it—that's a different story. It isn't easy to let go of the bush we're holding on to—no matter how insecure it may be—and just trust God. Many a person, when God has asked him or her for a full surrender, has looked around for a faith that didn't require that kind of commitment. It isn't easy to let go!

$\mathscr{A}$ Chain Reaction

May 21, 1946. The place: Los Alamos, New Mexico, at the dawning of the nuclear age.

Louis Slotin, a daring young Canadian scientist, was carrying out delicate experiments with uranium. He was helping prepare for the second atomic bomb test that was to be carried out in the waters of Bikini Atoll in the South Pacific. Slotin needed to determine exactly the amount of U-235 necessary for a chain reaction. Scientists called it the *critical mass*.

Slowly he pushed together two hemispheres of uranium. Then, just as the material became critical, he pushed them apart with an ordinary screwdriver, thus instantly stopping the chain reaction. He did this many times.

But on this day, just as the mass became critical, Slotin's screwdriver slipped! Instantly the room was filled with a dazzling bluish haze. Other scientists present jumped back in horror. But instead of ducking and perhaps saving himself, Slotin tore the two hemispheres apart with his bare hands. The chain reaction was interrupted.

By this instant, self-forgetful act of courage, Slotin saved the lives of the seven other persons in the room. He realized that he himself had been exposed to a lethal dose of radiation, but he retained his presence of mind. He shouted to his colleagues to stand exactly where they had been at the moment of the accident. He then drew on a blackboard a sketch of everyone's relative position. This would enable doctors later to discover the degree of radiation each man had absorbed.

A few moments later Slotin stood by a roadside, waiting with another scientist for the car that was to rush them both to a hospital.

Quietly, Slotin assured his companion, "You'll come through all right, but I haven't the faintest chance myself." That proved only too true. Nine days later, Louis Slotin died in agony.

Some two thousand years ago, the Son of the living God walked directly into sin's deadliest radiation. He allowed Himself to be touched by its curse. The accumulated guilt of the ages released its deadly contamination over Calvary. The Savior died in agony, but by His sacrifice He broke the chain reaction and destroyed the curse of sin.

A Fortunate Fall

A number of years ago a lighthouse was being built on the rockbound coast of Wales. With the building nearly completed, one of the workmen stumbled and fell from the scaffolding far down to the rocks below.

The other workmen, shocked at what had taken place, didn't dare look down for fear of being unnerved by the sight and then falling themselves. Heavyhearted, they backed slowly down the ladders, but to their surprise and happy relief, they saw their companion lying on a mound of grass, shaken and dazed. Bruised, to be sure, but not seriously harmed. Beside him lay a dead lamb. A flock of sheep had been grazing near the work site, and a lamb had broken his fall!

A Lamb has broken your fall. A Lamb has broken mine—the Lamb of God who takes away the sin of the world.

Blaming the Barometer

On September 21, 1938, a hurricane of monstrous proportions struck the East Coast of the United States. At the height of the storm, an immense wall of ocean water came crashing ashore between Babylon and Patchogue, Long Island, New York. That initial storm wave was so powerful that a seismograph in Sitka, Alaska, recorded the impact! The spray from that huge wave raced northward at more than a hundred miles an hour and whitened windows in Montpelier, Vermont, with brine!

For some reason, the meteorologists, who should have known what was coming and should have warned the public, seemed strangely blind to the impending disaster. Either they ignored their instruments or simply wouldn't believe what they were telling them. And, of course, if the fore-casters were blind, the public was as well.

Among the more unusual occurrences in this most unusual storm was the experience of a Long Island man who just a few days earlier had ordered a barometer from a store in New York City. The instrument arrived in the mail on the morning of September 21, just hours before the storm and the freak wave that would strike Long Island in the early afternoon. The man was irritated to see that the needle of the barometer registered below twenty-nine, where the dial indicated "hurricanes and tornadoes." Something was obviously wrong with the instrument. He shook it. The needle didn't move. He thumped it; he banged it carefully against the wall. Still, the needle remained fixed, pointing to "hurricanes and tornadoes." The man put the barometer back into its box, drove to the post office, and mailed it back to the store for a refund.

While he was at the post office, his house blew away in the storm!

That's the way we are sometimes. If we can't cope with the forecast, we blame the barometer. Or ignore it. Or throw it away.

$\mathcal{F}$orty Wrestlers

The story is told of a unit of the Roman legion encamped by a lake in Armenia in the dead of winter. At this time in Rome's history, it was a capital offense to turn away from the pagan gods and proclaim Christ. Forty of the commander's best soldiers had been found to be followers of the Lord Jesus and refused to renounce their faith in spite of everything that had been brought against them to make them recant. So, they were sentenced to die, banished out on the frozen lake.

Huddled together in the numbing cold, the little group of men began to sing. Their stern, pagan commander, watching from his comfortable tent, heard the words: "Forty wrestlers, wrestling for Thee, O Christ. Claim for Thee the victory and ask from Thee the crown."

Strangely moved, that hardened general, so used to cursing and frantic pleas for mercy, listened intently. These were men of his own company, men who had angered the authorities by their faith. These were his forty heroes, distinguished soldiers. Must they die?

He moved out into the cold, gathered driftwood from the shore, and built a huge fire with flames leaping high into the night. Perhaps this would lead them to reconsider their refusal and save themselves by giving up their faith in Christ.

But no. Again the sound of the refrain came to his ears, weaker now: "Forty wrestlers, wrestling for Thee, O Christ."

Then suddenly the song changed. "Thirty-nine wrestlers, wrestling for Thee, O Christ—"

As the song floated in across the ice, one of the prisoners climbed up on the bank and dropped by the fire, a shivering mass. The song of the forty was no more. One of the heroes had disavowed his faith.

On the shore, clearly visible against the fire, stood the commander. Strange thoughts surged in his heart. Suddenly, he took one brief look at the pitiful traitor before him and threw off his cloak. Before his soldiers could stop him, he raced down the bank and out across the ice to the freezing men, casting back the words, "As I live, I'll have your place!"

In a few moments the song, with a fresh note of triumph, came wafting back to the soldiers who had gathered now, fearful and awestruck, on the silent shore: "Forty wrestlers, wrestling for Thee, O Christ. Claim for Thee the victory and ask from Thee the crown."

The Ship That Wouldn't Burn

Have you heard of the wooden ship that wouldn't burn?

It was World War II. The place: the Marovo Lagoon in the Solomon Islands of the South Pacific where a British major had commandeered three mission schooners for war duty. When word came that the Japanese were approaching, the major gave orders for the three ships to make their escape. But the engine of the *Portal,* temperamental at any time, simply refused to start.

To prevent its capture and use by the enemy, the British major reluctantly ordered that the *Portal* be set afire. Immediately, a sheet of flame reached to the masthead, and the major, satisfied, left the scene.

What did the Christian islanders do? A hopeless situation? Not to them. They prayed that God would save their ship.

The flames were licking at the cabin and the rigging with fiendish glee when the fire went out just as if an invisible hand had snuffed out the flames enveloping the ship!

The local people, in their pidgin English, said, "*Portal* 'im 'e boat belong God 'im 'e no burn." And here was the proof.

As darkness approached, they maneuvered the ship into the mouth of a small creek and disguised it with foliage. But this was not all. To be sure the enemy could never use the ship, those local Christians took the engine to pieces bit by bit. They passed the pieces around to various individuals with the injunction that they guard them with care.

And they did—the kind of ingenious care that only they could contrive.

Some of the pieces of that motor were hung in trees. Some were hidden in the ground. Others became part of some native's wearing apparel. One boy was proud of a belt that he wore—composed of the nuts from the engine bolts. And one of the young women used several springs to hold her hair in place.

When the war was over, the *Portal* was again made sound and seaworthy.

And the engine? The word went out, "Marsta, 'im 'e want engine belong *Portal* one time quick!"

Almost immediately the bits and pieces began to arrive. Three weeks later, there was not so much as a half-inch screw missing from that engine assembly. The tank was filled with fuel, the engine boy gave the order, and almost as with a sigh of contentment, that temperamental engine sprang to life.

The ship that wouldn't burn. Life is full of surprises. But some of them have a reason.

No Lions!

You have probably heard of the man who walked the streets of New York City always snapping his fingers. Someone asked him why he was doing it, and he replied, "To keep the lions away." He was reminded that there hadn't been any lions on the streets of New York for a long time. And to that he answered triumphantly, "Effective, isn't it?"

Cooking or Eating?

A young pastor announced one day to his wife that he had decided to quit the ministry.

His wife was stunned, of course. But he explained, "There are problems in my life that I haven't been able to solve. I feel like a hypocrite. Until I can solve my own problems and doubts and questions, I'd better stop preaching."

At least he was honest!

But his wife suggested that before taking such a serious step he should seek counsel from an older, more experienced pastor. And he did.

As that devoted man of God began to understand the young pastor's situation, he leaned over and wisely said, "Son, go home and read the Book."

"What do you mean?" the young man asked in amazement. "I read it all the time."

The older man countered, "You don't understand. You prepare sermons just as a cook prepares food for the family, tasting it here and there to see that it is just right. But the cook must sit down and eat with the others—or die of starvation. You have been preparing for others. Now go home and read the Book for yourself."

The young man protested that he was too busy. But his friend persisted. "Take a day off and read one book of the Bible. Read it twenty times in one day. You'll see what I mean."

The young pastor went home thoroughly disturbed. He didn't like the idea any more than Naaman the Syrian liked Elisha's suggestion that he wash seven times in the Jordan River. It wasn't a very sophisticated prescription for his problem.

But his wife's counsel was reminiscent of the counsel Naaman's servants had given him. She said, "If he had asked you to do something difficult, you would have done it proudly. Why not try his simple suggestion?"

So, reluctantly, the young pastor took a day off and chose one of the shortest Bible books he could think of—2 Peter.

He and his wife read it through three times aloud. Four times; seven times. He knew then that he was a changed man. But thoroughly aroused, he continued. Ten times; eighteen times. They used every pen and pencil and crayon in the house to underline or circle words and phrases as new thoughts dawned on their minds. God's truth mellowed the young pastor's heart as deeper insights inspired him.

Finally they finished the nineteenth reading, and they were ready for the twentieth. "This last time we must read it on our knees," he said.

So, they took the Book to the bedroom. And there, kneeling beside the bed, they began to read. Then, as one more inspiration stirred his mind, a tear fell on the page. It fell where a pen had been used to underline a verse, and now there was an ugly blue stain. "Oh, look!" he said. "I've spoiled the page!"

But his wife answered, "No. The darker the page, the whiter your life!"

What is the power of the Book? What is its charm? What makes it so indestructible? It's the *Man* in the Book. It's the *Savior* it announces. It's the *Friend* it introduces. Read the Book. Read it for yourself. Read it to find forgiveness and victory. Read it to find a Savior, and you will not be disappointed.

Back to the Beginning

In 1772 one of those almost impenetrable fogs had settled down over the city of London.

In a dismal flat in the heart of the crowded East End, a man stood gazing into the fireplace. Then suddenly, overcome by emotions of discouragement and gripped by fears that he could not name, he threw his cloak about him and walked resolutely toward the door. He turned the key and walked out into the night.

Carefully he groped his way across the pavement and felt for the iron horse's head and the ring of the hitching post. Then, guided by the curbstone, he made his way to the nearest corner, where he knew a horse-drawn cab was always waiting.

He opened its door and ordered the driver, "To the Thames, sir!" For in his deep depression there seemed no way out but to jump from the bridge into the river.

It should have taken fifteen minutes. But after an hour and a half of negotiating the dark and foggy streets, they realized they were hopelessly lost. In desperation, he decided to walk and paid the driver his fare.

But as he alighted from the cab, his arm struck a familiar object. It was the iron horse's head of the hitching post that stood before his own door! After an hour and a half of fitful wandering, he had stepped down in front of his own home!

So impressed was he that he climbed the stairs to his flat, lighted the lamp, and knelt to ask God to forgive him for what he had thought to do. And then, there in that same room that had so lately overcome him with its gloom, he wrote these immortal words that Christians have been singing ever since:

God moves in a mysterious way
His wonders to perform;
He plants His footsteps in the sea,
And rides upon the storm.

Ye fearful saints, fresh courage take;
The clouds ye so much dread
Are big with mercy, and shall break
In blessings on your head. . . .

His purposes will ripen fast,
Unfolding every hour;
The bud may have a bitter taste,
But sweet will be the flower.

Blind unbelief is sure to err,
And scan His work in vain;
God is His own interpreter,
And He will make it plain.

Yes, it was William Cowper who learned that night something of the wonder of God's providence.

Truly Irreplaceable

Tom worked as a production technician in a television studio. He was often called upon to assist in the taping of special events. Tom was proud of his work; he understood the intricacies of television electronics well and had developed a special talent for troubleshooting during taping sessions.

One year Tom's union and the company he worked for couldn't settle on a contract. The union called a strike. Tom, along with the rest of the crew, walked off the job.

Tom didn't like the idea of just quitting. He felt uneasy sitting around the house. But he felt sure the company would settle on a contract quickly. After all, how could they get along without him and the other members of the crew? After years of experience, Tom had learned almost every detail involved in the production of a television program. Who else could they get with his expertise?

The strike, however, dragged on. The company didn't seem that desperate to compromise. And then Tom learned that he had been replaced. That was quite a blow—someone else filling his role. And what was worse, the company continued producing programs just as before. Tom had become dispensable.

His spirits plummeted. If he could be replaced so easily, how much did his life mean—what purpose could he really have? He wandered about the house aimlessly. But during this time of depression, Tom's family rallied around him. They comforted and encouraged him.

It was then that he began seeing himself in a new light. He looked again at those who depended on him day by day—his wife and children. And it dawned on Tom that there was one role in life no one but he could fill. There was one place where he would always be irreplaceable—in his family.

If Tom, the husband and father, went out on strike, no replacement would ever be found. No one else could have the same nurturing relationship he enjoyed with his wife and children.

Tom eventually went back to work and continued a productive career in television. But he no longer depended on his position for security. He understood where he truly was irreplaceable.

Oh, I know we all give lip service to the idea that our families are the most important thing in our lives. That's easy to say. But are you committed to fulfilling your one irreplaceable role? Or does your career crowd out time with the family? Does the pursuit of a promotion take priority over care for your wife or husband? Are you neglecting those closest to you?

The Miracle of the Chalk

The professor was no friend of God. And everybody in his five hundred-member class knew it. In September he had told them, "During the course of this semester all who have the desire to remain in this section of Anthropology 201 will learn the truth. In learning this truth, you will find every belief you have ever held about God or religion in general will be destroyed." And in the weeks that followed, the professor never missed an opportunity to criticize and ridicule religion.

Now the class was meeting for the last time before Christmas vacation. The professor was giving his annual lecture "proving" that prayer is a fallacy. He had been giving this lecture for ten years, so he knew it well. It had gone off so well the first time, and was such hilarious entertainment, that he had made it an annual event.

This day, as he finished his mocking attack, he stood up. He was wearing what he always wore for this performance—jeans, sneakers, and a T-shirt.

He glared at the auditorium full of students and defiantly inquired, "After two months in this class, is there anybody here who still believes in the ridiculous notion of religion?"

He walked around to the front of his desk. In his upraised right hand he held a new piece of chalk. The classroom had a concrete floor. All eyes were glued to the professor. There was utter silence.

Then with a mocking smile he went on with the challenge he had long since memorized. "Well, if there is anyone in this classroom who still believes in religion and the so-called power of prayer, I ask you to stand up and pray. Pray that when I drop this piece of chalk from my hand, it will not break. I defy you and this so-called power by stating that nothing—not all your prayers, not all your religion, not even your so-called God Himself—can stop this piece of chalk from breaking when I drop it. I defy you to prove me wrong!"

There was a slight movement near the right side of the auditorium. Every eye turned. A young man stood up and walked to the aisle. Then he moved toward the front and stopped in front of his instructor. "I believe," he stated in clear confident tones. "I still believe in God and in His power to answer prayer."

"Well," the professor responded, surprised. "How about this? We have before us a real, live person who claims he believes in this notion that God can answer prayer. Is that right?"

"Yes, sir. I know that God will answer my prayer."

"Just in case you misunderstood," the professor went on, "I'll explain to you again exactly what I am going to do." Then he went through the sequence again—how he would drop the chalk, how it would shatter into a dozen fragments, and how no power in the universe could keep it from doing so. Then he asked, "Do you still want to pray?"

"Yes, Professor, I do."

The professor reveled in this glorious moment of defiance. "All right, class, I want you all to be very quiet and reverentlike while this student prays." There was sarcasm in every word. Then he turned back to the young man. "Are you ready?"

And the student replied, "Professor, I've been preparing for this moment all my life."

"All right, then. We'll all be quiet and bow our heads while you pray." The words had lost none of their mocking, derisive tone.

Not one of the five hundred students could take their eyes off the young man. They held their breath as he turned his face heavenward and prayed, "God, I know You are real, and I pray in the name of and for the glory and honor of Your Son, Jesus. And I pray for myself, who trusts You with all my heart. If it be Your will, do not let this piece of chalk break when it hits the floor. Amen."

The smirk was still on the professor's face. "Is that it?" he asked.

"Yes."

The professor grasped the chalk in his right hand and held it up above his head. Then he let it fall. But that day a miracle happened. As the chalk tumbled toward the floor, it fell against the leg of his jeans. Then it toppled down onto his canvas sneakers, and with a muffled tinkle, it rolled to a stop on the concrete floor—unbroken!

The silence was deafening. Then a student somewhere burst into laughter. Soon another joined in. In seconds, the entire auditorium was filled with laughter at the red-faced professor. Someone in the back shouted to the young Christian who had prayed, "You did it!" The young man turned and smiled—a careful, humble sort of smile. Then he just pointed upward. And everyone understood. Even the professor.

Freedom Through Captivity

Robert Bartlett, the Arctic explorer, said that one summer he and his party brought back on their ship a large number of caged birds. About midway across the ocean, one restless bird escaped from his cage. In an ecstasy of freedom, the bird flew away from the ship, out across the water. They watched him until he disappeared in the blue of the sky. And they said, "That bird is lost."

But to their surprise, a few hours later, they saw that bird on heavy wing, coming toward the ship. Panting and breathless, the little feathered prodigal dropped upon the deck. How eagerly that bird, out over the water, had looked for that ship again! The ship was no longer a prison; it was home. The ship was the only way across the ocean!

And so, like that little bird, we batter and bruise ourselves trying to get away from God and fly off on our own. But we will find in the end that He is the only way across. "Make me a captive, Lord, and then I shall be free."

$\mathscr{H}$is Own Little Show

A friend of mine sat on the grass near the Washington Monument in our nation's capital. It was the Fourth of July. Every year a quarter of a million people gather there to watch one of the most impressive displays of fireworks to be found anywhere.

And what a spectacle it was this particular year! Showers of radiance. Thundering noise. Gasps of delight from the crowd.

As one especially brilliant fire cloud burst above the monument in a cascade of blues and reds and whites, my friend smelled a pungent whiff of smoke nearby. He turned to see a young man beside him lighting tiny sparklers that he had stuck in the ground. This person never saw the breathtaking fireworks against the ebony sky. Throughout the exciting fireworks spectacular taking place overhead, he tended his own little show and never looked up.

When the last rockets of the grand finale had faded from sight, my friend finally turned to leave—and almost stumbled over the young man. He was still there, elbows on his knees. Gazing vacantly at the smoking stubs of his burned-out sparklers!

What a picture of the spiritual condition of too many in our world today! Without Christ. Lost. Lost forever. Tending our little sparkler show while the grand display of God's salvation is painted across the sky above us!

The Power of Hope

Shawn Butler, a seven-year-old boy from Massachusetts, was dying of a cancer that had spread through most of his brain. He had been in and out of comas. He was weak and listless. On August 9, 1982, Shawn's father reluctantly agreed with his son's doctors that if Shawn stopped breathing, they would not attempt to revive him.

Then, four days later, Shawn received an unusual visitor—the boy's hero, Red Sox first baseman Dave Stapleton. Hearing Stapleton's voice, Shawn roused and actually talked to the man about baseball for a few minutes. Then Stapleton leaned over the bed and made Shawn a promise. "Tomorrow," he told the youngster, "I'm going to hit one over the fence just for you."

Shawn's eyes lighted up.

The following day, during the Red Sox game, when Dave Stapleton came up to bat, he had a determined gleam in his eye. And he smashed a pitch over the left-field wall for a home run!

Fast forward. Five months later, Shawn's doctors were baffled, completely confounded. They could find no trace of the cancer that had invaded almost all of his brain. The boy seemed to have recovered completely! He and his family began making plans for a trip to Disneyland.

What made the difference? No one knows for sure, of course. That's the way it is with miracles. But I believe that what made the difference for Shawn was a thing called hope. His hero had made a promise; they were connected. And so Dave Stapleton's home-run blast had become Shawn's great deed, as well. It had opened a door of hope in his hopeless case.

Yes, I believe that something as fragile as hope can make all the difference.

A Song in the Night

Elie Wiesel tells of a young Jewish boy, Juliek, who once gave a beautiful lesson in bearing witness to hope.

Elie met Juliek during a terrible night on the way to a Nazi death camp. He and hundreds of other Jews were forced into a barracks for three days in the town of Gleiwitz. They were jammed into a room so tightly that many actually smothered to death. The sheer mass of human bodies simply cut off sources of air.

Among these twisted bodies, Elie noticed one young emaciated Warsaw Jew—Juliek. He was clutching a violin tightly to his chest. Somehow, Juliek had managed to hang on to the instrument, mile after mile through snowstorms, during the forced march to Gleiwitz. Now he struggled to free his limbs. Crammed among hundreds of the dead and dying, he slowly drew his bow across the strings. And Juliek began to play a movement from a Beethoven concerto. The beautiful, lilting melody arose, pure and eerie in that horrible room.

In the darkness, Elie heard only those sounds of the violin. And he felt as if Juliek's soul were in the bow and his whole life were gliding on the strings. Elie would always remember the youth's pale, sad face as he played a tender farewell to his audience of dying men.

That night Elie fell asleep to a Beethoven concerto. In the morning he saw Juliek slumped over nearby, dead. Beside him lay his violin, broken and trampled.

But the song remained. Juliek's final melody still rose above the horrors of that death march. Not even Nazi cruelty could suffocate its gentle winsomeness. Juliek's song echoed the beauty of another world. It made an eloquent statement that there is something beyond all this sin and pain and misery we see so often in our world. Beauty and grace are what count in the end. These qualities will last forever.

Does your life express in some way the blessed hope? Have you found a song you can play—even in the darkest night?

Now Is the Time

In October 1871 the great evangelist Dwight L. Moody conducted a campaign in Chicago. At the close of his message one evening, he repeated the words of Pilate in that moment of procrastination: "What shall I do with Jesus?"

And then Moody said to his audience, "I wish you would take this text home with you and turn it over in your minds. Then next week we will come to Calvary and the cross, and we will decide what to do with Jesus."

Moody's song leader, Ira Sankey, began to sing. But his song was never finished. He was interrupted by the rush and roar of fire engines. Chicago was ablaze. And after the conflagration was over and great sections of the city were only charred and gutted ruins, Moody grieved, "Now I would rather have my right hand cut off than to give an audience a week to decide what to do with Jesus."

Time is crucial. Now is the time to make your decision. What will you do with Jesus?

The Prince of Peace

It was Christmas Eve 1914 during the horrors of World War I. British and German troops had dug miles of trenches in the French countryside from which they blasted each other with machine guns, mortars, and artillery.

Between the German and British trenches lay a barren no-man's-land, a narrow strip of craters and shattered trees where anything that moved was shot. Whenever there was a lull in the firing, the shivering men on both sides could hear the noise of cooking going on in the enemy trenches.

Late on Christmas Eve, with freezing rain still falling and the temperature dropping, a British guard heard a new sound wafting across no man's land. In the enemy trenches a man was singing, "Stille Nacht, Heilige Nacht." It was a tune the British sentry recognized as "Silent Night, Holy Night." He began to hum along with the melody. Then a second British soldier crawled over and joined in. Soon others on both sides began to blend their rough voices across the war-torn battlefield.

The German offered a second carol, "O Tannenbaum," and the British responded with "God Rest Ye Merry, Gentlemen." On and on through the night the singing continued. As dawn broke, signs appeared on both sides, in two languages: "Merry Christmas!"

Then, incredibly, one by one, the soldiers laid down their guns and crawled beneath the barbed wire into no-man's-land—scores of British and German troops meeting together. The soldiers opened their wallets and showed off pictures of their families and exchanged gifts of candy.

This experience, surely one of history's most remarkable occurrences on any battlefield, has come to be know as the soldiers' truce. Tragically, it was over all too soon. By midmorning Christmas Day, furious officers ordered their men back to the trenches. Soon the deadly bullets were whizzing back and forth once more. Later that day, a command came down from British headquarters forbidding such contact: "We are here to fight, not to fraternize!"

Nevertheless, for a few hours, the master of those soldiers was neither the kaiser nor an earthly king but heaven's Prince of Peace.

Holy Devil

The holy devil they called him—Rasputin, one of history's most riveting, yet revolting, characters. He was the peasant priest who wielded fatal control over Tsar Nicholas and the empress of Russia. What was the secret of his mysterious power?

Come with me to the old Winter Palace of the tsars in St. Petersburg.

Before the revolution of 1917, St. Petersburg was the capital of the Russian Empire. It became the stomping ground of Rasputin.

Rasputin—his very name has intrigued the world for decades since his death. The long-haired, wild-eyed peasant from Siberia has been immortalized in more than twenty movies, in addition to dozens of documentaries, miniseries, plays, and books.

Rasputin's rough-hewn appearance belied his role as favored guest of the royal court. He gloried in the contrast between his peasant mannerisms and the polished etiquette of the tsar's social circle. As he mingled with guests entering the palace wearing their fashionable furs, Rasputin thrust his coarse black tunic into the arms of the startled footman. Then, striding confidently into the crowded ballroom, the hulking thirty-three-year-old became the immediate center of attention.

He grabbed the hands of the noblemen and their wives with his own huge hands, gazing fiercely into their eyes. He interrogated them about personal matters, offering intimate advice. Flaunting his lack of education, he unabashedly belched forth crude language. He even plunged his unwashed hands into his favorite fish soup.

Incredible as it may seem, the uncouth peasant from Siberia charmed the hearts of St. Petersburg's social elite. His barbarian manners attracted rather than repelled his titled admirers. To them, he was an exotic diversion in a restless, shallow society.

One woman recalled her first encounter with Rasputin, as recorded in the classic biography *Nicholas and Alexandra*. "Our eyes met," she said. "His eyes held mine, those shining steel-like eyes which seemed to read ones inmost thoughts. He came forward and took my hand. . . . 'Thou are worried. . . . Well, nothing in life is worth worrying over. . . . It is necessary to have faith. God alone is thy help.' "

Rasputin embellished his conversations with ancient Russian proverbs and quotes from the Bible. He became a sought-after spiritual counselor, regarded as a holy man of God.

In reality, Rasputin was anything but devout. As a carousing young man, he had begun living the licentious, dissolute life which he continued the rest of his life. Returning from a pilgrimage to the Holy Land, he professed a dramatic conversion to Christianity and affirmed a fervent faith in Christ. But he never abandoned the wild orgies and drunkenness for which he had become a legend. How, then, did he manage to win the confidence of church leaders?

They saw an undeniable spiritual power emanating from his blazing, hypnotic eyes. And so the religious hierarchy of Russia endorsed Rasputin as God's servant to the royal family.

The peasant seemed to have the power of divine healing—and the royal family desperately needed healing when the tsar's son became ill. The boy suffered from an internal hemorrhage so serious that funeral arrangements were made. In that crisis hour a telegram arrived from Rasputin with the startling message: "The little one will not die." Immediately the bleeding stopped. Rasputin's prophecy came true.

The aunt of Tsar Nicholas testified, "There is no doubt about [Rasputin's healing powers]. I saw those miraculous effects with my own eyes, and that more than once. I also know that the most prominent doctors of the day had to admit it."

Empress Alexandra and Tsar Nicholas became convinced beyond question that Rasputin must be God's messenger—how else could he work such miracles? Before long the wild peasant through his healing power virtually controlled the royal family. The fall of the Russian Empire was not long in following.

One historian concluded, "The fatal influence of that man [Rasputin] was the principal cause of death of those who thought to find in him their salvation."

Some Christians automatically assume that any supernatural power must come from God. But the case of Rasputin raises some troubling questions. Some miracles are the work of Satan done in the spirit of lawlessness, violating God's law. Despite his claim to holiness, Rasputin trampled on the Ten Commandments. Ladies of the court fell prey to his adulterous advances. This supposed holy man urged the women to go ahead and sin with him. He assured them that only after they indulged in sin could they appreciate the blessing of forgiveness. Countless women succumbed to Rasputin's seduction—after all, he had miraculous powers, so he must be from God, they reasoned.

They should have known better. Rasputin's contempt for the Ten Commandments betrayed his satanic sponsorship.

Rasputin forged his stranglehold upon the Russian Empire by winning the blessing of church leaders. Father John of Kronstadt and the saintly

Bishop Theophan, two of the most revered priests in Russia, endorsed Rasputin's ministry. They were deceived by his fervent "faith" and his ability to work miracles.

As time went on, however, the priests had second thoughts. They heard the embarrassed confessions of women led into sin by Rasputin. The priests, being men of integrity, were horrified. Convinced at last that Rasputin's debauchery disqualified him from being a man of God—despite whatever miracles he could perform—they urged the empress to banish the monster.

But the damage had been done by the priests' previous endorsement of Rasputin. Instead of exiling his carousing "holy man," Tsar Nicholas dismissed Father John. Rasputin boasted, "I have shut his trap!"

God's Word warns, "There is a way that seems right to a man, / But its end is the way of death" (Proverbs 16:25). Rasputin's evil ways brought about his untimely death at the age of forty-four. He was drowned the night of December 30, 1916.

The fateful rendezvous took place after five Russian nobles, distressed about Rasputin's stranglehold on the empire, met to plot his death. They determined to poison him in the cellar of Moika Palace. The bait for their trap was the promise of a party with Princess Irina, famous for her beauty, someone Rasputin longed to spend time with.

On the night of his death, the assassins welcomed Rasputin at the palace. With the tune of "Yankee Doodle Dandy" playing happily upstairs, Rasputin ate several poisoned cakes, washing them down with poisoned wine. Although the food had enough potassium cyanide to kill an ox or two, the amazing priest didn't drop dead! He just seemed a bit dazed.

The assassins wondered what to do about their uncooperative victim. For the next two hours or so, they entertained him with music. Finally they lost patience with their poison and shot him through the heart.

A physician on the scene pronounced Rasputin dead. But then, horror of horrors, his eyes fluttered open, and the hulking maniac roared to life. Furious, he lunged at his would-be killers, chasing them out into the snow-covered courtyard.

There he was shot several times. Finally his assassins tied him up in a blue curtain and dragged him to the bank of the Neva River. Rasputin was thrown into the icy river where he finally drowned!

Not long after Rasputin's death came the fall of the empire he had led into perdition. Later, Tsar Nicholas and his family were arrested. The night of July 16, 1918, the royal household met its bloody fate. It was the result of following the evil priest—a tragic forecast of what will happen to all who pursue spiritual deception.

The Bible warns that in the last days the devil will work miracles in the name of Jesus. So let's reject anything or anyone who operates outside of harmony with God's commandments. Only then can we be secure from the final deceptions of the enemy.

Pulling Down the Stars

An unbeliever, so the story goes, was doing a little boasting. He said to a Christian, "We're going to destroy all your churches and burn all your Bibles. We won't leave you a thing to remind you of your God."

The Christian said nothing. He only looked up toward the sky and smiled. The boaster was annoyed. "Why are you smiling?"

"I'm just wondering," said the Christian, "how you're going to get the stars down!"

Thousand of years ago, the psalmist wrote, "The heavens declare the glory of God; / And the firmament shows His handiwork" (Psalm 19:1).

Just a Drink of Water

Northern California was in the grip of a heat wave. It was camp-meeting time. In those days everyone lived and cooked and slept in tents at camp meeting. And tents were stifling in the heat. Even so, the campers had crowded into the big pavilion to hear one of their favorite speakers—Pastor Luther Warren. Among them was a mother with two small children. And, of course, the children were restless.

Finally, the charming little two-year-old fell asleep in her mother's arms. The older child was blue-eyed with slightly curling blond hair. The mother was eager to hear the message and tried patiently to help the child at her side to sit quietly. But it was so hot, and the folding chair was so hard. Soon came the inevitable request—a drink of water.

The mother waited, reluctant to disturb the sleeping child. Then suddenly the little girl pointed vaguely in some direction. "There's a man over there who has a drink of water!"

In those days it wasn't dangerous for a child to ask a stranger for a drink—especially at camp meeting. The mother gave her permission, telling the little girl to be sure to come back right away. Then she settled back and relaxed. Maybe now she could listen to the message.

Suddenly, with unbelieving eyes, she saw her small daughter walk right up on the platform and ask the speaker for a drink! She sat transfixed as she saw Pastor Warren stop and pour a glass of cold water from the pitcher that had been placed on the pulpit. And the child expressed her thanks by lifting her blue eyes to gaze into his.

If you ever knew Luther Warren, you would know that he didn't mind the interruption a bit. Instead, it gave him the perfect opportunity to talk about cool, invigorating water—on a hot, thirsty day.

" 'If anyone thirsts,' " Jesus said, " 'let him come to Me and drink' " (John 7:37). And he told the woman at the well, " 'Whoever drinks of the water that I shall give him will never thirst. But the water that I shall give him will become in him a fountain of water springing up into everlasting life' " (John 4:14).

Ragtag and Bobtail

In the earliest days of Christianity, the pagan critic Celsus jeered at Jesus. Scornfully, he called Him the strangest of teachers. Why? Because "while all the others cry, 'Come to me, you who are clean and worthy,' this singular Master calls, 'Come to Me, you who are down and beaten by life'; and so, being taken at His word by these impossible people, He is followed about by the ragtag and bobtail of humanity trailing behind Him."

To this accusation, the Christian scholar Origen gave a devastating reply. "Yes," he said, "but He does not leave them the ragtag and bobtail of humanity; but out of material you would have thrown away as useless, He fashions men, giving them back their self-respect, enabling them to stand up on their feet and look God in the eyes. They were cowed, cringing, broken things. But the Son has made them free."

Living Like a Sheep

Suppose a timber wolf should watch a flock of sheep and admire the habits of these peaceful animals. Suppose he decides that this is the way an animal should live and that from now on he will live just as a sheep lives. Wouldn't that wolf have a difficult time living like a sheep? Wouldn't he be likely to slip back into his old wolflike way of life? Grass might seem quite tasteless as he remembered feeding on some carcass.

But suppose that God, by some miracle known only to the Creator, should transplant into that wolf the nature of a sheep. Then would it be difficult for him to live like a sheep? Not at all!

That is exactly what God has promised to do for you and me. "If anyone is in Christ, he is a new creation; old things have passed away; behold, all things have become new" (2 Corinthians 5:17).

Witnessing for the Master

Boris Kornfeld was a Jewish medical doctor accused by Stalin of some political offense and imprisoned at a former concentration camp outside Ekibastuz. As Charles Colson remembers in his outstanding book *Loving God,* Dr. Kornfeld became a Christian while in prison. Quietly, he began witnessing for Christ.

One day he sat beside the bed of a young man suffering from intestinal cancer—and an obvious spiritual malady even more serious. The patient, shaking with fever, missed much of the good doctor's testimony of faith. But he understood enough that afternoon to be impressed with the possibility of freedom in the Lord Jesus Christ.

Late that night, with the guardhouse lights glaring outside, Dr. Kornfeld summed up his confession with the whispered words, "On the whole, you know, I have become convinced that there is no punishment that comes to us in this life on earth which is undeserved."

The patient realized he was hearing an amazing admission. This man was a persecuted Jew who once considered himself innocent. Now he proclaimed that everyone deserves to suffer—but, thank God, Jesus Christ took our place on Calvary's cross. Jesus suffered in our place. By accepting His sacrifice, we can stand clean before God, bound for eternal life in heaven.

The young patient drifted off to sleep that night with Dr. Kornfeld's testimony resounding in his heart. Early the next morning he awakened to the sound of commotion. During the night, someone wielding a hammer had attacked Dr. Kornfeld as he slept.

As the doctor was carried to the operating room, where he died, his patient opened his heart to a new life in Jesus Christ. "God of the universe," he cried, "I believe You!" And the gates of heaven opened wide to that repentant sinner, imprisoned there within the gates of hell.

That young man lived to leave the gulag and tell the world his story. He became one of the most important moral voices of modern times—Alexander Solzhenitsyn. The world may never honor the name of the Jewish doctor who witnessed for Christ in that dark gulag, but millions of Christians today thank God for Solzhenitsyn's testimony.

How Did It All Come About?

Probably nowhere else in the world is there such a blend of catastrophe and creation, of violence and calm, of chaos and exotic beauty as in Hawaii. So, it's not surprising that the early Hawaiians, the Polynesians, tried to explain their strange new world as they explored these islands of the Pacific.

They came to believe that Pele, a goddess from their ancient homeland of Kahiki, was responsible for the volcanic activity of their new home. One story has it that in Kahiki, the goddess had failed to show respect for the sacred land and had burned it, so she was expelled by her brothers. She came north to the little island of Kaula and tunneled into the earth but found no place where her fire could be sustained. Next she traveled southeastward, always hoping to find a deep hole where her fire would take hold. On the island of Maui she dug the great crater of Haleakala. But again she had no lasting success. So, at last she crossed the water to the island of Hawaii. Here she found Kilauea and was satisfied. So the pit of Kilauea, a nearly always active—or at least smoldering—caldera, is said to be the home of the fire goddess Pele.

The ancient Hawaiians believed that the goddess needed to be appeased when she became violent. So, even today, when there is an eruption, you might see a Hawaiian throw twigs of ohelo or a red handkerchief into the caldera to appease the anger of the ancient deity.

There is another tradition that concerns Haleakala, on the island of Maui, which last erupted some time after 1750. *Haleakala* means "house of the sun." According to Edward Joesting, writing in the book *Eternal Hawaii,*

> Tradition has it that Maui, the trickster demi-god of all Polynesia, was annoyed with the sun which sped too fast across the sky. His mother, Hina, had difficulty drying the bark-cloth, or kappa, she made. The days were too short to provide sufficient warmth.
>
> So Maui devised a plan. He knew that the golden shafts of light seen early in the day were the sun's legs. One by one, as they appeared through the clouds at the top of Koolau Gap, he snared them and bound them fast to an ohia tree. The sun, thus, entrapped, pleaded for release, but Maui relented only after the sun promised to slow his daily march.

Of course, Hawaii isn't the only place on this planet that seems to demand an explanation of its past. All over this earth there are phenomena we don't fully understand. Sheer escarpments, boulders tumbled in chaotic formations, fossils of marine life high in mountain ranges, erosion channels where they don't seem to belong—all have one message: something happened here!

What happened? What were the forces that created these things? Are our explanations more credible than those of the ancient Hawaiians?

Not long ago a Sequoia National Park ranger strolled into a crowd of about three hundred people who had made the climb from Owens Valley to the granite summit of Mount Whitney. One of the hikers, simply awed by the sight of the two-mile plunge down to the valley floor, asked the ranger how the Sierra Nevada came to be shaped as it is.

The ranger had had a smattering of geology, and he replied, "Well, this summit plateau is part of the old landscape that was lying here as a kind of rolling lowland millions of years ago. Then the whole Sierra was bowed up like an arch." More people turned to listen, and he went on, "Then the keystone collapsed to form this great escarpment going down into the Owens Valley, with the White Mountains over there to the east making the other half of the broken arch. And later, through erosion and glaciation, we got the final shaping of the land—the meadows and canyons and peaks and bowls as you see them all around you today."

The ranger paused to let all that information soak in, and one of the hikers spoke up. "I don't believe anything you say. The Bible says the Lord made the world in six days, so nothing you say is true!"

Now, the outspoken hiker might have more logically pointed to the convulsion of the earth at the time of Noah's flood as a better explanation. For the question being discussed was not how the Sierra came to be but how it came to be shaped as it is. But the ranger didn't challenge the hiker's faulty logic. The real issue was the reliability of the Bible record. And evidently the ranger had no inclination to challenge the hiker's rebuttal—at least not at the moment. Instead, he replied thoughtfully, "Well, yes, it does say that." And he wandered off by himself to think about it. Months later he hadn't thought of a more suitable reply. "What could I tell the guy?" He shrugged. "Besides, maybe he was right!"

Yes, the hiker could have been more tactful. But it's true that the Bible tells us all we really need to know about our past. And it may be that even the Sequoia National Park ranger realized that the account we find in the

Bible is far less complicated, far more reasonable, far easier to believe than the popular but changing theories of the geologists who probe among the rocks for answers.

Unable to Forget

The rebellious planet would like to forget God. It denies His existence and questions His dealings and quibbles about His words. It alternately buries Him and resurrects Him! But it seems strangely unable to put Him out of its mind!

Why all this preoccupation with God? Why all this talk about God by men and women who don't believe in Him? Is there a hunger within the hate?

These questionings are like the Russian girl who was brought up as an atheist. She had just written a government examination and, like all students, was concerned about some of the answers she had given. The question that troubled her most was this: "What is the inscription on the Sarmian Wall?"

She had written, "Religion is the opiate of the people." But she wasn't sure that was correct. So, she walked the seven miles to the Sarmian Wall and checked. There it was: "Religion is the opiate of the people." In her relief she forgot her atheism and exclaimed, "Thank God! I had it right!"

They are like the girl who says of her boyfriend, "Oh, we're not speaking anymore. I've lost all interest in him. We haven't spoken for three days, six hours, and twenty-three minutes!" Not speaking anymore. But just try to get her to more than ten feet from the phone!

That's this planet. Through with its God. Not speaking anymore. But forever listening for His ring!

A Matter of Identity

The story is told of an airline pilot assigned to international flights. Since he had several days off between work assignments, he had time for other interests and purchased a small service station.

One day, in need of some small items, he dropped in at the hardware store up the street. His purchase completed, he stopped to chat about something of interest on his last flight overseas.

When he had gone, another customer asked, "Who is that man?"

And the owner replied, "Oh, he has a service station down the street here." And then with a smile, "He thinks he's an airline pilot!"

Most of us have only indulgent smiles and little compassion for the man who is confused about his own identity. We put him in what we consider to be an appropriate pigeonhole, along with the man who thinks he's Napoleon, and go on our way. But sometimes we are the ones who are confused, and we make some embarrassing mistakes.

It was no different in the days of Jesus. Some thought He was confused. Others wrote Him off as an impostor, even a blasphemer—for Jesus did claim to be God. But the matter of His true identity refused to be put to rest. What if He was telling the truth? What if He really is God?

Twisted Thinking

In 1974 a militant political fringe group kidnapped Patty Hearst, nineteen-year-old granddaughter of the famous, wealthy newspaper baron William Randolph Hearst. Nothing bad had happened to her before. Now she was locked in a closet, blindfolded for fifty-seven days—tortured, interrogated, and raped. Her captors repeatedly threatened her with death. They forced her to participate in a bank robbery. Now a criminal wanted by the FBI, she became convinced that she could never go home again. Convinced that this was the end. Convinced that she was finished and that the FBI would shoot her on sight—or if they didn't, that her captors would. So desperately convinced that she was finished that she might as well give up and join the group that had kidnapped her!

In fact, Patty Hearst was so convinced that all was hopeless that even when she had opportunity after opportunity to escape, the thought never entered her mind to try!

Eventually she was captured and arrested in September 1975. She served twenty-two months in prison before being released.

Barbara Walters, an experienced reporter, interviewed Patty Hearst and pressed her—almost merciless at times—with the questions that were on everyone's mind at the time: "Why didn't you just surrender to the authorities?" "Why did you behave the way you did?" "You had many opportunities to escape. . . . Why didn't you?" "You were alone for several days. . . . You could have picked up the phone and called your parents. Why didn't you do that?"

And the answer? "It never crossed my mind."

We can't understand. We can't understand why someone does not do what we think we would have done under those same circumstances. We are so sure that in the same situation we would have grabbed a phone in seconds or let out a bloodcurdling scream that could be heard for blocks or raced to the nearest police officer. And we are certain that once we were free, in the friendly hands of the police, we wouldn't have clenched our fist in a gesture of loyalty to the "revolution" (as Patty did) and given our occupation as "urban guerilla" (as Patty did). It wouldn't have taken us a week to realize that we "didn't have to say those things anymore" in order to survive.

We're so good at asking questions—and measuring the answers by our own unkidnapped thinking.

But Jesus understands. He understands the kidnap victim. He understands that we have all been taken captive by Satan and sin. He understands the sinner and the twisted thinking that sin can set up in our minds. He understands you and me.

Sundar Singh

Cyril J. Davey tells the story of Sundar Singh, a boy of India. He was almost fourteen when his mother died and his world collapsed. He was desolate. No one could comfort him. He knew he could not live without God. But it seemed to him that God had taken away the only person who could ever make Him real.

Sundar attended a Christian mission school because the government school was too far away. He had always been a quiet and courteous student. But now everything changed. Now, in his grief, he became a violent young ruffian. The kindness of the teachers only infuriated him. He hated them. He hated their school. He hated their Book. And he hated their Jesus!

One day he approached one of his teachers and politely asked to buy a New Testament. Little did anyone suspect why he wanted it.

Soon he was saying to his young friends, "Come with me. You are surprised that I should buy this Book. But come home and see what I do with it! How long I shall live I cannot tell you. Not long, certainly, but before I die I will show you what I think of Jesus and His Book!"

He led the way to the courtyard of his home, brought a bundle of sticks and a tin of kerosene, and set the wood burning. Then slowly and methodically, he tore the pages from the Book one at a time and threw them on the fire. He wanted it to be his last gesture of contempt for the Christians' Book!

Suddenly his father walked out of the house and thundered, "Are you mad, child? Are you beside yourself to burn the Christians' Book? It is a good Book—your mother has said so. And I will not have this evildoing in my house. Stop it! Do you hear? *Stop it!*"

Sundar bent down, stamped the rest of the New Testament into the flames with his foot and went to his room without a word. He stayed there for three days and nights.

Then came the night that was to decide it all. He knew what he would do. Not far away he heard the sound of a train as it rushed toward Lahore and was gone. The next express would be at five o'clock in the morning. And if God had not spoken to him before then, he would go out and lay his head on the rails and wait for the train from Ludhiana to Lahore to end his miserable existence.

His mind must be clear this night. He went to the bathhouse and bathed in cold water for an hour before returning to his room. It was seven hours until the express would come through.

He prayed, "Oh, God—if there be a God—reveal Yourself to me before I die!"

The hours passed.

At fifteen minutes to five he rushed into his father's room and grabbed the sleeping man by the shoulder. "I have seen Jesus," he burst out!

"You're dreaming, child," his father said. "Go back to bed."

But Sundar was not dreaming. He told his father how he had planned to end his life—and rushed on with his story.

"A few minutes ago," he said, "Jesus came into my room. . . . And He spoke to me. . . . He said, 'How long will you persecute Me? I have come to save you. You are praying to know the right way. Why do you not take it? I am the Way.' "

Sundar continued, "He spoke in Hindustani, and He spoke to *me!* I fell at His feet. How long I knelt I cannot say. But when I rose the vision faded. It was a vision. It was no thought of mine that called Him there. . . . Had it been Krishna or one of my own gods, I might have expected it. But not Jesus!"

His father spoke sharply, "You *must* be mad. You come in the middle of the night and say you are a Christian. And yet it is not three days past that you burned the Christians' Book!"

Sundar stood rigid, looking at his hands. Then he said with deep feeling, "These hands did it. I can never cleanse them of that sin until the day I die!"

No wonder he loved Jesus! No wonder he preached Jesus till the day of his death! No wonder he made his way, almost every summer, into the forbidden land of Tibet, enduring the cruelest persecution. But the more he was persecuted, the happier he was that he could suffer for his Lord. From his last trip into Tibet, he never returned.

*A*n Ancient Spinmaster

Public relations is not an art that has emerged only in recent times. Ramses II, of Egypt, was an ancient spinmaster who could have competed successfully with any modern public relations guru.

Ramses reported the Battle of Kadesh as only a skirmish in which he, of course, was wildly victorious. The reality was that the Battle of Kadesh turned out to be much more than a mere skirmish, and Ramses, rather than being the victor, barely managed to escape with his life!

On the massive pillars and palace walls of mighty Karnak, Ramses described again and again his conflicts with the king of Hatti. The Assyrians also frequently mentioned the land of Hatti. But historians did not guess the truth for many years. They assumed that the Hatti were only some unimportant tribe. No one thought to ask how an unimportant tribe could continue to skirmish with two great powers—Egypt and Assyria—for so many years. The Hatti turned out to be not a tribe at all but a third giant empire of that day—the Hittites, whose borders stretched from the Black Sea to Damascus!

But no matter, Ramses was equal to the public relations challenge. At least we must give him credit for putting on a bold front.

One of Ramses' Egyptian inscriptions concerning the Battle of Kadesh described him as the "fearless one" who "put an end to the boastfulness of the land of Hatti." He was "the son of Re who trampled the land of Hatti underfoot." He was like a "bull with sharp horns," "a mighty lion," "the jackal who in a moment traverses the circuit of the earth." He was "the divine, splendid falcon." He also composed a long poem describing his tremendous victory.

Today it is known that these claims were shameless propaganda. Yet, Ramses was believed for three thousand years!

The truth of the battle is that Ramses allowed himself to be taken in by the story told by two Bedouin spies that the Hittite king sent into his camp. These men, claiming to be deserters from the Hittite army, told Ramses that the Hittite king had already retreated from him in fear. Always susceptible to flattery, Ramses allowed his army to fall into the Hittite trap, escaping only with his life.

A neat trick, isn't it? Lose the battle, but convince the world that you won. And succeed in perpetuating your version of events for three thousand years.

The Battle of Kadesh was fought around 1300 B.C. The chief of the fallen angels—Satan—suffered a defeat around A.D. 31—a defeat infinitely more important than the Battle of Kadesh. At the cross Jesus won a great victory, and it could be said that Satan barely escaped with his life. But the devil has managed to put a spin on what happened at the cross that has fooled thousands and millions of people ever since. Comparatively few understand what took place at Calvary. Comparatively few have accepted the salvation that Jesus offers as a result of His victory over Satan at the cross. At the cross, sin and Satan were defeated. God and salvation won a great victory. And now, Jesus offers to you and me the fruits of that victory if we will only accept it.

Pride Turns Itself In

The Salem witchcraft trials of 1692 splashed a blot on American history. But what happened afterward should make us proud.

Today only a gaunt oak tree marks Gallows Hill, the spot where twenty innocent victims, during three months of trials in 1692, were executed as witches and buried without ceremony in common graves.

It was a time of hysteria in Salem, Massachusetts. Satan himself seemed to have descended on the town. At least a good many people were accused of being in league with him. Something like one hundred and fifty people were said to be witches and were tried in court. Scores were imprisoned. Twenty were executed. Salem was determined to be free of witches!

It all started when a number of teenage girls were caught playing forbidden games of magic. This, in the Puritan atmosphere of those days, was considered very serious. So, when they were discovered, the girls panicked. They screamed, they trembled and threw themselves to the ground.

When they saw that their elders were much impressed by their strange behavior, the quick-thinking youngsters decided they had a good act going. So, they continued it. Here was a way to escape punishment.

The doctor was called. He said he couldn't do anything for them. The ministers were called. And the ministers said that the girls were bewitched.

The misbehaving teenagers continued their act. If they were bewitched, someone must be bewitching them. So, they began to accuse various members of the community. The older people, of course, were their targets.

The youngsters proved their accusations, at least to the satisfaction of their elders, by falling into fits and writhing on the floor whenever the accused person touched them or even looked at them.

And so the hysteria grew. Suspicion was in the air. There were more and more accusations. There were court trials. There were excommunications. There were hangings!

So it was in 1692. But as the hysteria died down, the Puritan conscience began to work. The people of Salem began to see what they had done. They saw that innocent people had been put to death at their hands. Salem repented!

And Salem knew that true repentance leads to confession!

Just five years after the tragic hysteria, Samuel Sewall, one of the judges of the witchcraft trials and who later became chief justice, made a public apology. He stood humbly at his pew in the church while the minister read his confession. He said he desired "to take the blame and shame of it, asking pardon of men, and especially desiring prayers that God, who has an unlimited authority, would pardon that sin."

Think of it! A public confession from a judge. But that wasn't all. The jurors published a confession signed by all twelve men, saying they feared they had been guilty of shedding innocent blood.

The minister, Samuel Parris, issued a statement expressing his repentance and asking pardon. But even that did not satisfy the members of his church. He was dismissed from his post.

Chief justice of the witchcraft court was William Stoughton, who had been a strong supporter of the trials. But it was he who, as acting governor, signed a declaration setting aside a day of fasting for the community to express repentance for the witchcraft wrongs.

Ann Putnam, the ringleader of the girls who had made the accusations, made a public confession. She said she had accused persons she now believed to be innocent. And she said, "I desire to lie in the dust and be humbled for it in that I was a cause, with others, of so sad a calamity to them and their families."

Salem was caught up in repentance as it had been in the campaign against the supposed witchcraft. Excommunications were reversed, property restored, names cleared, a monument erected to the memory of Rebecca Nurse, one of those who was hanged. Every group in the community made some gesture of apology—even witnesses and bystanders.

Evidently, Salem's repentance was deep and genuine. It made its confession public because its sin had been public. And it did everything possible to undo its wrong. True repentance will never do less.

Confession is a great and noble thing. It isn't easy. Guilt always prefers to remain hidden. It balks at turning itself in. It takes real courage to stand up and say, "I was wrong." But how many things might be different, how many wounds healed, how many names cleared, how many lives made happy—if, in private and public life, we had more of such greatness!

"If we confess our sins, He is faithful and just to forgive us our sins and to cleanse us from all unrighteousness" (1 John 1:9).

Justice and the Judge

Some years ago an incident happened in a California courtroom that helps us to understand how God deals with sin. A young woman was given a ticket for speeding and brought before a judge. The judge read aloud the citation and said, "Guilty or not guilty?"

She said, "Guilty."

The judge brought down his gavel and fined her one hundred dollars or ten days in jail. But then he stood up and took off his robe. He walked around in front of the desk—and paid her fine! He was her father!

Now, why didn't the judge just say to his daughter, "You've broken the law, but I love you so much that I forgive you"?

He couldn't—that is, he couldn't do that and be a good judge, a just judge. He had to uphold the law. But he could pay the fine himself.

So it is with God. Heaven's law has been broken, and the penalty is not a hundred dollar fine. It is death. No matter how much God loves us, He can't just say, "I forgive you" and let it go at that. Heaven's perfect law, the foundation of His universe, must be upheld. To do otherwise would mean chaos. God couldn't downgrade the law or disregard it or change it or alter it or dispense with it or overlook it—not even to save the life of His own dear Son.

So don't let anybody ever tell you that Jesus died on the cross to do away with the law—that the Ten Commandments were nailed to the cross. It was just the opposite. If the law could have been changed or re-vised or overlooked, then Jesus didn't need to die—and Calvary was only a meaningless drama.

Jesus died on the cross because there was no other way to save you and me—except to die in our place, except to die Himself.

Wouldn't it be unthinkable not to accept a sacrifice like that? Wouldn't it be unthinkable not to ask for, and accept, a forgiveness that cost so much?

Faithful in All Things

The siege of Leningrad (now St. Petersburg) was one of the most ter-rible ordeals of death, suffering, and tragedy of World War II. For 890 days—from September 1941 to mid-January 1944—the brave citizens of this Russian city had withstood famine, artillery, and bombardment from the air. The soldiers defending the city and the citizens died by the thou-sands and tens of thousands. In all, an estimated 750,000 perished from starvation, freezing, or battle.

But out of the horror of Leningrad's nightmare comes the thrilling story of Maria Vladimirovna. You can read it in the thought-provoking book *Parting With Illusions,* by Vladimir Pozner, a leading commentator during the days of the Soviet Union. Pozner met Maria in the 1960s while writing for a Soviet magazine. He saw the plainly dressed elderly woman checking visitors' handbags at the State Hermitage Museum's Gold Treasure Room.

None of the visitors would have suspected that humble Maria had been born to a Russian nobleman, an admiral in the navy of Tsar Nicholas. She spent her childhood years at the Winter Palace surrounded by the splendor of the Hermitage. After the Bolshevik Revolution, the new Soviet government appointed Maria as a caretaker of the Hermitage Museum. Year after year she faithfully, quietly performed her duty. Then came the day Hitler's invasion interrupted business as usual. All too soon the German *wehrmacht* was pounding on the gates of Leningrad, vowing to exterminate the city.

In that crisis hour, the director of the Hermitage Museum summoned Maria for a top secret assignment. "Leningrad may fall," he sadly acknowledged. "We're evacuating our entire collection of painting and art. But there is something else—the gold treasures, the unique works of ancient Greeks . . . they are priceless. I want you to supervise their packing. And once the crates are ready, you will oversee them being loaded onto trucks and have them buried in a secret destination."

Solemnly he charged her: "Maria, you alone will be responsible. Those treasures will be yours until we defeat Hitler and restore them to our beloved city."

Well, that was quite an assignment for Maria. For four long years she lived in a tiny village somewhere in the Far North, suffering like everyone else from the cold, hunger, and poverty. Yet, at her disposal were millions worth of gold, gems, and other treasures. Who would have noticed the loss of one or two diamonds out of thousands of them?

But when the glad day came when the gold treasures returned to the Hermitage, not one jewel was missing. Maria had been faithful to her trust. And from that day to her death, she continued watching over them. The thousands of visitors whose bags she checked never suspected that this humble little woman had preserved for them the national treasures.

Maria is no longer living, but her legacy remains. Paul says of the gospel, "We have this treasure in earthen vessels" (2 Corinthians 4:7). Each of us has been entrusted with its safekeeping and with preserving it for future generations. Are we as faithful to our trust as Maria was to hers?

You Can't Keep It to Yourself

A doctor once found a little dog with a broken leg by the roadside. He took the little fellow home, cleaned him up, set the broken bone, and put a little splint on it to hold it in place.

The little dog loved the doctor. He followed the kind man around the house and around the yard—until the leg was well. Then suddenly he disappeared. *That's gratitude,* thought the doctor. *As long as he needed me, he stayed. But as soon as he didn't need me any longer, he ran away.*

But the doctor spoke too soon. For the very next day there was a scratching at the back door, and there was the little dog. Back again, wagging his tail. But beside him was another little dog. And that other little dog was lame!

Yes, that's the way our life in Jesus grows. That's the way it is with our love for the Master. You can't keep it to yourself. It must be shared.

The Missing Chapter

Classics in religious books are few and far between. Not many are enduring enough to achieve that status. But I have one in my library that I prize very much. It was written in the 1800s by a Quaker, Hannah Whitehall Smith. It's called *The Christian's Secret of a Happy Life.* My 1952 edition says that two million copies had then been sold. It's still selling.

But imagine my surprise to discover recently that a chapter is missing from my copy of the book.

I owe this discovery to Catherine Marshall, wife of the famed Peter Marshall. She, of course, became an author in her own right. Catherine Marshall, too, had prized this book for many years. But in 1970 someone gave her a very old copy of the book—an 1885 edition. And as she paged through it, she was surprised to find that it contained a chapter that has been deleted from later editions. It was a chapter about the Holy Spirit.

Why had the publishers left it out? What was wrong with it? Naturally, she was curious. And when she had read the chapter, she was even more curious.

She found nothing dangerous or extreme or unorthodox in the missing chapter. There is nothing unorthodox about a belief in the Holy Spirit, for the Holy Spirit is the Third Person of the Godhead—just as truly God as the Father and the Son. And there is nothing wrong with the desire to be filled with the Spirit, baptized with the Spirit, for that is taught in Scripture.

Hannah Smith's chapter was filled with Scripture and with common sense. She said the baptism of the Spirit should not be thought of as a single experience but as a life. She warned that the baptism of the Holy Spirit "means far more than emotion. It means to be immersed or dipped into the Spirit of God, into His character and nature. The real evidence of one's baptism [by the Spirit] is neither emotion nor any single gift such as tongues, rather that there must be Christ-likeness in life and character: by fruits in the life we shall know whether or not we have the Spirit."

She wasn't ruling out emotion, you understand. She said that the baptism of the Spirit can be, though it isn't always, a very emotional and overwhelming sense of His presence.

What could be wrong with such a sensible and balanced presentation as that? Catherine Marshall was now determined to find out why the publishers had felt it necessary to delete it. And she turned up a very interesting story.

It seems that in 1865 Hannah Smith moved to the village of Milltown, New Jersey, along with her husband, Robert, and their children. There Robert took charge of a branch of the family glass business. And Hannah met a group called the Holiness Methodists.

Some of the most perceptive and valuable parts of the book she would later write, *The Christian's Secret of a Happy Life,* came from insights she gained from this group. In her book, she was able to present their ideas in everyday words that anyone could understand.

Eventually, Robert was as caught up in his wife's interest in the Holy Spirit as much as she was. One summer the Smiths went to a ten-day Holiness camp meeting on the New Jersey coast. They came, as Hannah said, "to open our hearts to the teachings of the Holy Spirit," but it was Robert, rather than his wife, who experienced an extraordinary emotional encounter with the Spirit.

Here is how Hannah described what happened to her husband: "After the meeting my husband had gone alone into a spot in the woods to continue to pray by himself. Suddenly, from head to foot he was shaken with what seemed like a magnetic thrill of heavenly delight, and floods of glory seemed to pour through him, soul and body, with the inward assurance that this was the longed-for baptism of the Holy Spirit."

She went on to say, "The whole world seemed transformed for him; every leaf and blade of grass quivered with exquisite color. . . . Everybody looked beautiful to him, for he seemed to see the Divine Spirit within each one. . . . This ecstasy lasted for several weeks and was the beginning of a wonderful career of spiritual power and blessing."

Naturally, this made Hannah desire a similar experience. She went to the altar night after night. She prayed for hours on end. But nothing happened. Not then, nor ever, did she have an emotional experience such as had come to her husband.

At first she was disappointed. Then she realized that God had already given her a revelation of His character that had changed her life. She had wanted emotion. But God had given her fact—something more permanent and substantial.

But the story isn't over. In 1873 the Smiths moved to England, where their lives were intertwined, by marriage or by friendship, with such names as Bertrand Russell, George Bernard Shaw, and others of the elite of England. For years the Smiths conducted a very successful lay ministry among the aristocracy.

And then in the spring of 1875 Robert Smith traveled to Germany, where he held highly successful evangelistic and teaching meetings before large crowds, always in a highly charged emotional atmosphere. In a letter to his wife he exulted, "All Europe is at my feet!" When engraved pictures of him were offered for sale, eight thousand sold immediately.

At the height of all this attention and success, the blow came. There began to be rumors of Robert engaging in improper conduct with female admirers. Whether or not these rumors were true was never proved—then or later—but the gossip continued. The emotionalism that Robert found so appealing had apparently gotten out of hand.

The press picked up on the story and spread the rumors of misconduct. Sponsors in England canceled future meetings. For a time, the Smiths returned to New Jersey. Through all this, Hannah quietly supported her husband. She wrote a friend about "the crushing blow" that had befallen Robert.

And the blows did crush him. He became discouraged, disillusioned, and somewhat cynical. Slowly, he sank into a joyless old age, while his wife, who had never depended on emotionalism in her walk with the Spirit, continued to maintain her trust in God's leading. Her deep, quiet faith sustained her through trials and difficulties.

Tragedy came to Robert Smith when he gave in to the temptation to exalt emotion and an ecstatic experience over a faithful worship of the Lord Jesus. No ecstasy was apparent with his wife. Instead, Hannah Smith's balanced view of God and the Holy Spirit gave her a firm, happy, quiet confidence.

And the missing chapter in her book? What about that? Evidently, after Robert's experience, the editors felt it was safer to omit this chapter on the Holy Spirit. They were afraid that the fire of emotionalism that had burned Robert might do the same for readers if they left the chapter in the book.

This story has something to tell us today, as well. Too great an emphasis on emotion, too little attention paid to the great truths of God's Word, too little emphasis on purity, honesty, morality—Christ living in us—all these things will result in spiritual decline.

Aren't we on dangerous ground when we try to measure the genuineness of our conversion or of our continuing walk with Christ by the amount of emotion accompanying it? Shouldn't we see warning signs when we make feeling the *goal* instead of the *by-product*—when we make feeling an end in itself?

There is nothing wrong with emotion in religion. But emotion needs intelligent control. It needs discipline. A person who has had an experience with the Lord Jesus Christ ought to be different from the way he or she was before. And if not, if our lifestyle is still the same, then our spiritual experience ought to be suspect.

Emotion is not the big thing in life. Living counts too—everyday living in the power of the Holy Spirit and the love of Jesus Christ.

A Variation on a Miracle

The story is told of a new Christian whose faith in the Bible was challenged by his former drinking buddies. "We don't believe Jesus really turned water into wine," they scoffed. "How do you know such miracles really happened?"

For a moment the new believer wondered what to say. Then he quietly replied, "I admit I can't prove Jesus turned water into wine two thousand years ago. But I can tell you this. In our home, He turned my six-packs of beer into furniture for my family."

Praise God, He can work miracles in your heart and in your home too!

The New Age and the Future

A strange sound welcomed the dawning day on Mount Shasta. The eerie chant dipped and rose over the chilly slopes as forty young Californians stretched their arms toward the rising sun. Then, holding hands around a circle, they began humming, along with five thousand other celebrants on the mountain.

Unusual happenings are nothing new in California, but this was more than typical summer madness. "Harmonic convergence," they called it. All over the world that Sunday, New Age believers gathered in thirty-six spots they consider sacred. In places such as the Grand Canyon, the pyramids of Egypt, and on Mount Fuji in Japan, they met to welcome a New Age of peace and love.

For months the New Age devotees had been studying ancient prophecies of the North American Indians, linking them with the sun worship calendars of South American Maya and Aztec Indians. They concluded that a special alignment of planets and constellations on Sunday and Monday, August 16 and 17 of 1987, would produce cleansing energy for our planet.

New Age believers saw a unique opportunity—this was supposedly the first time in 23,412 years that the heavens had poised themselves in such a blessed position. Emile Canning, the group leader on Mount Shasta, implored, "One hundred forty-four thousand sun dancers filled with the sun will bring on the New Age. Allow yourself to become one of the one hundred forty-four thousand, one of the dancing suns." World peace and relief from catastrophe would result.

The New Agers got their numbers that Sunday—more than the required one hundred forty-four thousand sun dancers. But their hopes for a New Age failed them. That very night Northwest Airlines Flight 255 crashed in Detroit, Michigan, the second-worst single air disaster in the history of the United States as of that time. Hardly what New Age believers expected from their incantations!

The weekend also passed without the massive UFO sightings some had predicted. Probably the closest thing to an alien visit was reported by one of Shasta's residents: "We're seeing a form on our television that looks like something like a dove with two widespread wings—we can't explain it."

Well, perhaps a TV repairman could.

Or maybe not. Something more than the ridiculous was happening. The New Age movement had joined hands with the spirit world. Events of the weekend included "channeling," where famous departed personalities supposedly disclosed their harmonic wishes through psychic mediums. In a meadow beneath Shasta's fir-covered slopes, two hundred pilgrims from Los Angeles paid thirty-five dollars each to listen reverently as the apostle John (from Bible times, you know) spoke to them through a channeler named Gerry Bowman. Or so they imagined.

Actually, all of us can know what the apostle John has to say—and it won't cost us thirty-five dollars to find out. In his Gospel in the New Testament, John quoted the words of Jesus: " 'In My Father's house are many mansions; if it were not so, I would have told you. I go to prepare a place for you' " (John 14:2). Then, John says, Jesus promised, " 'I will come again and receive you to Myself; that where I am, there you may be also' " (verse 3).

What a wonderful eternity we will have in the Lord Jesus Christ! This new age, the Bible explains, begins with Jesus' coming in power and glory. Picture the glorious scene! The Son of God piercing the vaulted heavens, moving down the star-studded highway of the skies, attended by myriads of angels. Then He calls out with a voice of thunder, "Awake, you that sleep in the dust of the earth! Arise to everlasting life!"

And loved ones you have lost will hear. That voice calling the dead will be heard around the world. Families will be reunited. Children snatched away by death will be placed again in their parents' arms! What a reunion day!

Cruising to Armageddon

A week or so after Inauguration Day in 1977, President Carter's national security advisor decided to run a test. He had been briefed on plans for protecting the president in the event of an attack on Washington, D.C. So Brzezinski went to the officer in charge. With a smile he asked if the man really could get the president out of the city and out of harm's way before the missiles came in.

"Yes, sir," the man answered. "That's why I'm here."

"Have you practiced?" Brzezinski wanted to know.

"Of course, the officer proudly assured him. "We test this system all the time."

"That's good, because the president authorized me to do just that." Brzezinski then pushed back his left sleeve and pressed a button on his watch. "Pretend I'm the president. Pretend an alarm has sounded indicating a nuclear attack. Get me to safety."

"Now?" the officer stammered.

"Now!" Brzezinski pushed the button again, and the seconds began to fly.

The officer protested, "You can't mean now. It's dark. It's snowing. It's—"

He was cut short by a look that stunned him. He babbled a series of breathless orders into the phone.

Brzezinski then dashed for the back lawn of the White House to meet the rescue helicopter. On the way outside he grabbed a secretary to play the role of the first lady.

The helicopter should have been ready to go when he arrived, but three precious minutes went by as they waited. Five minutes. Finally, it dropped down to take them away.

Airborne at last, Brzezinski began testing communications. "Call the Joint Chiefs of Staff," he ordered. And the crewman put the call through the White House switchboard.

"Don't bother to continue. If this were really an attack, that switchboard would be demolished by now."

So it went. It took twice the allotted time to reach the big jet that would whisk the president away to safety. Known as the doomsday plane, this elaborately modified 747 stands by on constant alert, ready to take off in three minutes. It wasn't.

One thing more. This little test easily could have been Mr. Brzezinski's last flight. For the officer in charge was so nervous and confused that he forgot to alert the Secret Service guards. They almost shot down the escape helicopter as an intruder!

The news report of this incident was titled "Cruising to Armageddon."

Armageddon! The word sends shivers up our spines. Just the mention of it sparks all kind of fearful speculation. Does anyone know what will happen during the showdown of Armageddon?

Whatever Armageddon really is, it seems we aren't quite ready for it.

Armageddon, the Bible says, is a showdown between truth and error, loyalty to God or loyalty to the powers of evil. At its core, Armageddon is a spiritual conflict. And it involves every human being personally. To each of us comes the challenge: Will we obey God's covenant of grace? Will we be counted among those who loyally keep His commandments.

Yes, we all have a part to play in Armageddon. When God overcomes the powers of evil, we can overcome with Him!

Amazing Grace

After Chuck Colson was released from prison where he had been sentenced for his role in the Watergate scandal of the Nixon White House, Colson didn't forget the men and women still behind bars. One day in 1981, with a team from his Prison Fellowship ministry, he was visiting the Indiana State Penitentiary. As Colson recalls in his book *Loving God,* the group made its way through the maze of concrete cellblocks to the double set of barred doors leading to death row. The warden opened the individual cell doors, and one by one the condemned men timidly ventured out to mix with Colson and his volunteers.

Colson shared a brief message from the Bible; then all of them joined hands to sing "Amazing Grace." Following prayer, Colson's group said Goodbye to the prisoners and began filing out. They were crowding into a caged area between two massive gates when they noticed that one of their number was missing. Colson went back to get the man.

This volunteer, a short white man in his early fifties, was standing shoulder to shoulder with a young black man, reading together from a Bible. "I'm sorry. We have to leave," Colson urged, glancing at his watch. After all, the schedule was tight. Outside, a plane was waiting to whisk Colson to a meeting with the governor.

The volunteer looked up. "Give us just a minute, please. This is important," he said softly. Then he added, "You see, I'm Judge Clement, the one who sentenced James Brewer, here, to die. But now he's my brother, and we want a minute to pray together."

Colson recalled, "I stood frozen in the cell doorway. It didn't matter who I kept waiting. Before me were two men: one was powerless, the other powerful. One was black, the other white—and one had sentenced the other to death. Anywhere other than the kingdom of God, that inmate might have killed the judge with his bare hands—or wanted to, anyway. Now they were one in Christ, their faces reflecting an indescribable expression of love as they prayed together."

On the way out of the prison, Judge Clement told Colson that every day for four years since he had sentenced Brewer to death, he had been praying for his salvation. Thank God, those prayers had been answered.

Yes, James Brewer was a saved man there in death row. Both judge and condemned prisoner stood clean before the Lord, equal in God's sight—equally lost outside of Christ, equally saved in Christ. You see, heaven comes to us not because we are worthy but because we have entrusted our lives to the Lord Jesus Christ, who died for us on Calvary's cross.

The amazing grace of God that saved Judge Clement and James Brewer is your only hope—and mine, as well. What's more, the same transforming grace that united the hearts of those two courtroom foes can renew your relationships too. There is power in the amazing grace of God.

Welcome Home!

Some years ago a boy quarreled with his father and left home. His parting words were bitter and rebellious: "You'll never see me again!"

Three years passed—three tough years. He wanted to go home, but he was afraid. Would his father let him come back? He wrote his mother and told her he would be on a certain train as it passed the house. He asked her to hang something white in the yard if it was all right with his dad to come home.

The boy was nervous on the train. He sat in one seat and then another. A minister noticed and asked what was wrong. The boy poured out his story. They rode along together as the boy looked out the window. Suddenly he jumped up excitedly. "Look, sir, my house is just around the next bend. Will you please look for me? Please look and see if there is something white in the yard. I can't stand to look for myself."

The train lurched as it rounded a slow curve. The minister kept his eyes focused. Then forgetting his dignity, he shouted, "Look, son, look!"

There was the little farmhouse under the trees. But you could hardly see the house for the white. It seemed those lonely parents had taken every white sheet in the house, every bedspread, every tablecloth, every dish towel, even every handkerchief—everything they could find that was white—and hung them out on the clothesline and on the trees!

The boy stared, and his lips quivered. Before the train had completely stopped at the water tank, he jumped out. The last the minister saw of him he was running up the hill as fast as his legs could carry him—toward the sheets fluttering in the wind, toward home.

That's how God feels about you. He longs for you to come home.

An Everyday Hope

Erasmus, the great scholar of the sixteenth century, related an experience that shows what hope can mean in our everyday lives. It happened during a sea voyage. The sailing vessel Erasmus was traveling in ran aground. As violent waves smashed against the ship and it began to break up, even the sailors panicked. The passengers were nearly hysterical. Most shouted for help to their patron saint, sang hymns, or pleaded loudly in prayer. Paralyzed by fear, they hoped for some kind of supernatural intervention.

Erasmus noticed one passenger, however, who acted very differently. "Of all of us," Erasmus later wrote, "the one who remained most composed was a young woman who was holding a baby whom she was nursing. She was the only one who did not shout, weep, or bargain with heaven. She did nothing but pray quietly to herself while clasping the baby tightly on her lap."

This prayer, Erasmus realized, was just a continuation of her regular prayer life. She didn't ask for any exceptional favors. She seemed to trust herself entirely to God.

As the ship began to sink, this young mother was placed on a plank, given a spar to use as an oar, and sent out into the waves. She had to hold her baby with one hand and try to row with the other. Few thought she would survive the pounding surf.

And yet, her faith and composure stood her in good stead. The woman and her child were the first to reach shore.

Erasmus would never forget that young mother's calm demeanor in the face of death. She wasn't clinging to any desperate human efforts. The only hope worth having was the hope that had sustained her all her life— the hope and trust that God Himself would provide.

Never Forsaken

Let me tell you about Noble Alexander, a twentieth-century hero of faith.

His government would have left him alone if he had lived his faith silently. But now, this young Christian man insisted on leading souls to Jesus. So, the authorities imprisoned him as a *plantado*—a rebel against the revolution.

Noble's ordeal began innocently enough. One day the police pulled over his car and politely requested, "Would you mind coming with us to headquarters? We'll keep you only five minutes."

Well, those five minutes turned out to be twenty-two years! More than two decades of suffering. For forty-two days they subjected him to Chinese water torture. Then they starved him for six weeks, demanding that he abandon Jesus Christ. After Noble refused to work on the Sabbath, they plunged him, with his Adventist friends, into a pool of raw sewage. Four Sabbaths in a row he and his friends worshiped God, up to their chins in that slime, singing hymns of praise. Finally the guards let them keep the Sabbath in peace.

Somehow Noble smuggled a Bible into the prison, and every night the prisoners gathered for worship. Catholics, Baptists, Pentecostals, and Adventists prayed and sang together, united by their common faith in Christ.

Noble Alexander remained in prison until 1984, when Jesse Jackson negotiated his release and deportation to the United States. I had the privilege of meeting this remarkable Christian. Let me tell you that after all this man had suffered, he was one of the most cheerful, delightful people I've ever met.

The Lord who sustained Noble Alexander will be with you in whatever trials and difficulties you may be experiencing. He has promised never to leave us or forsake us. He will be at our side until the glorious day when He bursts through the clouds to take us home.

Waiting for the Genuine God

In 1867 a Norwegian missionary named Lars Skrefsrud came to India to live among two and a half million people called the Santal. They lived in a region to the north of Calcutta.

Lars demonstrated a great ability as a linguist. He soon became so fluent in Santal that people came from miles around just to hear this foreigner speak their language so well. And so Lars began to talk about Christ's great kingdom to these people. He explained the good news of salvation.

Now Lars, like many missionaries, wondered how many years it would take before these people, so far removed from any Christian influence, would show an interest in the gospel, how long it would take for them to open their hearts to this very different good news.

To Lars's amazement, the Santal were immediately electrified by what he was saying. After a while, one of their leaders exclaimed, "What this stranger is saying must mean that Thakur Jiu has not forgotten us after all this time!"

Lars caught his breath, astonished. Because he knew that *Thakur* was the Santal word for "genuine" and that *Jiu* signified "god." The genuine God? Lars realized he was not introducing some new concept to the Santal by talking about the one supreme God.

And so he asked, "How do you know about Thakur Jiu?"

The Santal replied, "Our forefathers knew Him long ago."

Lars then asked, "Since you know about Thakur Jiu, why don't you worship Him instead of the sun, or worse yet, demons?"

The Santal faces around the missionary grew wistful. "That is the bad news," they replied. And then a Santal sage stepped forward and said, "Let me tell you our story from the very beginning."

He proceeded to tell a history of how humankind had become alienated from the one true God—a story that, amazingly enough, paralleled the Bible story.

"In the present age," the sage said, "it is said by some that the sun god is Thakur. But the forefathers taught us that Thakur is distinct. He is not to be seen with fleshly eyes, but He sees all. He has created all things. He has set everything in its place, and He nourishes all, great and small."

Lars listened with growing excitement. Here a people had been prepared to receive the good news, just as the Jews were prepared by their sacrifices and ceremonies to receive Christ as the Messiah. The missionary discovered that generations of Santal children had grown up hearing their elders exclaim, "Oh, if only our forefathers hadn't made that grievous mistake, we would still know Thakur Jiu [the genuine God] today! But as things stand, we've lost contact with Him."

Almost before Lars realized what was happening, he found himself with thousands of inquirers on his hands, begging to know how they could be reconciled to Thakur Jiu through Jesus Christ. They were thrilled by the thought that their sins could be forgiven, that the rift between themselves and the genuine God could be healed.

And healed it was. Soon Lars was reporting back to Europe as many as eighty baptisms a day. Converts began to reflect Christ's character. And they bravely took the gospel still further among their own people.

The good news bore good fruit. In Lars's Santal mission alone, eighty-five thousand believers were baptized, and many other missions were created to evangelize and train those who had been waiting so long for Thakur Jiu.

Satan has spread his empire far and wide. He deceives and seduces and bullies people into his evil empire. But God is at work on our planet too. He has planted seeds in people's hearts all over the world that wait to sprout and bloom under the gentle care of a loving witness.

Who Was It?

It happened in Scotland during World War II. A young woman received the dreaded notice that her husband was missing in action. At first she clung to the hope that perhaps he'd be found, that maybe, just maybe, there had been a mistake. But months passed; no further word came, and finally this woman realized that her husband wouldn't be coming back.

Then several friends, who had contact with a spiritualist medium, urged her to attend a séance and try to make contact with her deceased husband. The thought of being able to see and talk with the one she loved and needed so desperately had an irresistible appeal.

The young woman attended the séance. Contact was made; she recognized her husband's voice! During subsequent séances they talked over many things only the two of them could have known about.

And then one day this woman answered a knock on her door—and almost fainted to find her husband standing there—in the flesh, alive and well. There *had* been a mistake; he hadn't even been seriously wounded, much less killed.

Well, you can imagine the joy of that reunion. But imagine the wife's perplexity also. To whom had she been talking all this time? Lying spirits had taken advantage of her loneliness. This woman gradually grew bitter and disillusioned with all religion.

There is only one hope for breaking through the grave, only one way to eternal life. There is only One who has conquered death for us. Jesus Christ is the one and only Source of eternal life.

Overcoming by the Blood of the Lamb

Standing just beyond Hadrian's Temple in Rome is the place where the empire of Christ began. It is a most unlikely place for the beginning of a worldwide empire—the Roman Colosseum. That is where the early Christian martyrs shed their blood in the name of Jesus Christ. They refused to pay homage to Caesar in Hadrian's Temple; they would not bow down to the emperor as to a god. They stood against a religion that used the state to enforce its dogma.

The empire of Christ began on the floor of the Colosseum, in silent testimony before forty-five thousand Roman citizens yelling for blood. Today, we see only the underground cells where prisoners and wild beasts were kept, awaiting their fate. Back then, the floor of this amphitheater turned crimson with the blood of those who proclaimed their allegiance to Christ alone.

Thousands of believers were burned alive, crucified, or killed by wild beasts. Their testimony rang out loud and clear: allegiance to Jesus is more important than life itself. Their suffering was a silent protest against the religion of conquest, the religion of state power.

The bodies of the Christians were taken out through a small gate, the *Porta Libitinaria,* named after Libitina, the Roman goddess of death, and were carried quickly away for burial in unmarked graves—pathetic corpses seemingly insignificant compared to this great colossus of Roman might.

But the martyrs' testimony proved stronger than the sword of Rome. Their blood watered the seeds of faith in many other hearts. They became conquerors. The apostle John explains their triumph over Satan and his evil empire this way: " 'They overcame him by the blood of the Lamb and by the word of their testimony, and they did not love their lives to the death' " (Revelation 12:11).

Eleni's Legacy

Greece, that cradle of democracy, has had its share of bloody struggles down through the centuries. During the 1940s, a civil war tore apart the nation already suffering through the bloodshed of World War II.

One of the tragic victims of this violent period was a woman named Eleni. She saw that the guerillas in Lia, her tiny village, were forcing the teenagers to join them in their fight. And there was talk that they were planning to send the younger children away for "reeducation." So, this young mother determined to save her children.

Eleni planned an elaborate escape. Unfortunately, a fellow villager betrayed her. Eleni managed to get her children out to safety, but she had to remain behind.

When the local guerilla leader, a man named Katis, found out that Eleni had helped her family to escape, he was furious. He interrogated Eleni and had her tortured.

Then he gathered the residents of Lia together for a "people's trial." Katis read a long statement charging that Eleni was a known fascist. He also accused her of undermining the efforts of the guerillas by organizing escapes from the village.

When neighbors stood up to defend Eleni, Katis promptly cut them off. He and two other judges retired for a few minutes and then returned. Katis announced that the evidence against Eleni was overwhelming, and she was sentenced to death.

A few days later, Eleni and several other condemned villagers were taken up into the hills to the execution grounds. Eleni stumbled along on legs black and swollen from torture. She looked thin and pale, near death.

But as one villager recalled, she mustered enough strength, just before the rifle shots rang out, to utter a terrible, piercing cry: "My children!"

Nicholas, Eleni's son, grew up remembering his heroic mother who had managed to save her children at the cost of her own life. He had been nine years old when his mother died. Over the years, he determined to find out all he could about her execution. He flew to Greece several times and visited the village of Lia and talked to villagers there about their memories of the civil war. Slowly he began to piece together the story of how his mother had died. And through this he discovered the identity of her murderer, Katis.

Nicholas traced the man to the town of Konitsa. He decided to go there and find him. All the others directly involved in his mother's mock trial and execution were now dead. Only Katis remained, the man behind it all.

As Nicholas drove a rented car toward Konitsa, he thought of his mother's final cry—"My children!" He had agonized for some time about how to understand those heart-wrenching words. Had his mother met death with acceptance, willing to defy a human command to honor a higher law of the heart? Or was she crying out for vengeance?

Nicholas arrived at the home of Katis and was invited in by his wife. After a few words of introduction, Nicholas said, "There was a trial of civilians in Lia in which you took part."

"No, no," Katis replied. "I tried no civilians."

"There were three hundred villagers present," Nicholas answered. "They remember you."

Katis became very nervous and continued to deny everything. Nicholas pressed his accusations, his outrage mounting before this hard, unrepentant man. He clutched a revolver in his pocket, ready at the least provocation to kill the one who had heartlessly tortured and murdered his mother.

But then Nicholas realized that if he killed Katis, he would also have to kill his wife and a grown daughter who was in the house. Otherwise, he would never get away.

Nicholas abruptly left and slammed the door behind him. There was no doubt in his mind now that Katis deserved to die. Justice demanded it. He had seen the arrogance and the cold indifference of a killer in the man's eyes. Nicholas vowed to confront the man again, this time when he was alone.

Four months later, Nicholas found his man vacationing in a port on the Ionian Sea. Nicholas waited outside Katis's apartment until he saw the wife and daughter leave and head toward the beach. Then he forced the lock open on the front door and slipped inside. There in front of him lay the executioner, fast asleep. This was it. The moment he had been waiting for. Nicholas wouldn't even have to use his gun. He could just smother the old man. The family would return and find that Katis had died in his sleep. No one would suspect anything.

Nicholas stepped forward. But then the memory of his mother overtook him—her gentle touch, her loving words. Nicholas had learned much more about her since he'd begun investigating her tragic death.

One witness told him that on the day before her execution, Eleni did not speak of the pain of her torture but only of her longing to embrace her children one last time. That's what she lived for; there was little room in her life for hatred.

As Nicholas stared at his mother's murderer, he realized that her final cry—"My children!"—had not been a curse on her killers. It had been an invocation of what she had died for, a declaration of her love.

And at that moment Nicholas wanted Eleni's love to live on in him and in his children. He didn't want the cycle of injustice and vengeance to continue. Nicholas was able to look past the killer to his victim and see the beauty of his mother's sacrifice. He turned around and walked out of the house, closing the door softly behind him.

Friends, that's what God's judgment is all about. It's not an opportunity for vengeance. It's an opportunity for God's beautiful sacrifice to shine forth. We have a heavenly Father who cries out, "My children!" That's what He lives for. There is no room for hatred in His heart. He has given His life for each of us. Love compelled Him to make the ultimate sacrifice. We have been purchased by the shed blood of God Himself. We are His cherished children!

Forgiveness Isn't Cheap

What do you say when someone asks you to forgive a wrong? Do you say, "Oh, there's nothing to forgive"? Or "Forget it. It was nothing"? Or "I didn't even notice it"?

You may recall the old legend of the ox and gnat. The gnat had been riding on one of the ox's horns. After a while the gnat said to the ox, "Excuse me. I didn't realize that my weight might be a burden to you. Please forgive me."

And the ox replied, "I didn't even know you were there."

Is that the way we make people feel sometimes when they ask us to forgive them? They may have been weeping under a burden of guilt. And when they come to us for forgiveness, we pretend to be so big, so noble, so perfect that nothing they could do could possibly hurt us; we didn't even notice.

Sin hurts. A wrong done to another hurts. Jesus never said, or even intimated, that sin doesn't hurt. It does. It hurts terribly. Jesus' heart bleeds with the pain of every wrong. He never said it doesn't hurt. He just says that He is willing to bear the hurt Himself.

That is what forgiveness is. It means that we are willing to bear the hurt ourselves. Forgiveness isn't cheap. And we will never truly realize what forgiveness involves until we understand what it cost. Forgiveness is the costliest thing in the world, in the universe. It cost the lifeblood of the Son of God.

Don't Think of the Red-Faced Monkey

An Indian fakir came to a village declaring he would demonstrate how to make gold. The villagers gathered around as he poured water into a huge caldron, put some coloring matter into it, and began to repeat magic words as he stirred.

Then distracting the villagers' attention for a moment, he let some gold nuggets slip down into the water. After stirring a little more, he poured off the water, and there was the gold at the bottom of the caldron.

The villagers' eyes bulged. The town moneylender offered the fakir five hundred rupees for the formula, and the fakir sold it to him. "But," he told the moneylender as the exchange took place, "you must not think of the red-faced monkey as you stir. If you do, the gold will never come."

The moneylender promised to *remember* what he was supposed to *forget*. But try as hard as he could, he could never keep the red-faced monkey from sitting at the edge of his mind, spoiling all his gold!

Concentrating on your sins will get you into trouble. Keeping your eyes on Jesus will keep you out of it.

An Unusual Rescue

Awhile back, a most unusual rescue operation took place two twenty-four hundred feet above an airport near the border of Austria and Hungary. A twenty-six-year-old skydiver—an experienced parachutist with 586 previous jumps to his credit—was stepping out of the door of the plane when he tripped over some ropes. The ropes caught hold of his legs and held them inside the plane, but allowed the rest of his body to fall outside.

He couldn't climb back in. Nor could he get loose. And the pilot couldn't help. He was alone at the controls and running low on fuel. He faced either remaining in the air and running out of gas or trying to land with the skydiver still hanging from the door of the plane.

Friends on the ground saw the predicament. One of them took off in a light plane, carrying a hunting knife with him. He flew close to the plane in trouble and managed to throw the knife to the parachutist, who caught it and cut the ropes around his legs. He was then able to drop away from the plane. His parachute opened, and he landed safely!

What a rescue!

That's our predicament. We're caught in the ropes of sin. We can't get loose. We can't get out or in. We haven't anything with which to cut the ropes that hold us.

But, yes, we do have something that will cut the ropes and set us free. The Lord Jesus, at tremendous risk to Himself, came to this planet to rescue us. He has tossed us a knife, and it's a sharp one. It's the Word of the living God, "sharper than any two-edged sword" (Hebrews 4:12).

This Book is not only sharp; it is powerful. It's full of promises—promises that are meant for you and me personally. You can claim them by faith, and they will cut you loose from the sins that bind you.

*L*ast Man at Bat

It was the last game of the playoffs—the New York Yankees and the Kansas City Royals. The game would decide which team would play in the World Series. Kansas City had held the lead through most of the game and was finding it difficult to hold back the celebrating of its first pennant till the game was over. But the Yankees came back to tie the score and then took the lead in the top of the ninth. And the Yankees went on to win the game and the championship.

Television cameras showed the winning players in the Yankee locker room—jumping up and down, hugging each other, hilarious with joy. But for viewers it was a sad picture. For another camera was projecting across the bottom of the screen—below the happy scene—one lone player for the Kansas City Royals. There he was alone, forsaken, in the Royals' dugout, sitting motionless with his head buried in his hands, heartbroken.

The player was Freddie Patek. He had been hurt earlier in the game but had gone back in. He had been the last man at bat. Everything depended on him—the game, the championship. And he had hit the ball. But the Yankee defense had executed a double play, and the game was over. Patek had done his best, but it hadn't been enough. If only he had hit a home run!

That's the tragedy of competition. When one teams wins, another team must lose.

But, thank God, the Christian life is not that way! According to God's rules, everybody can win who wants to win, who chooses to win. You can win. I can win. Not because of a brilliant performance on our part but because of an incredible sacrifice on the part of our Lord. And because we are willing to take His hand and trust him completely, He will lead us home.

Identifying the Real Jesus

Ernest Digweed was a retired teacher. He lived alone in a small house in Portsmouth, England, and had no known relatives. A neighbor said he "didn't dress or look like a wealthy man, kept very much to himself, and hardly ever spoke to anyone." He was eighty-one when he died in 1976.

But it turns out that he left a rather strange will. He left forty-four thousand dollars for Jesus Christ on the occasion of His return to earth.

And Mr. Digweed wanted to be sure the money didn't go astray. So, he specified that Christ, in order to claim the money, must return within the next eighty years. He must return specifically "to reign on earth." And He must prove His identity to the British government. There are those who think that may not be so easy to do.

His probate attorney said, "I certainly anticipate we are going to have a lot of trouble, particularly with cranks." And he asked, "Who can tell us who is the real Jesus Christ? Different people think different things."

Personally, I don't think Jesus will ever collect the money—or make any attempt to collect it. But on this matter of identity, I have the distinct impression that when Christ returns, it will be we—not He—who will have to produce identification. And for some of us it will be difficult—in fact, impossible. Some of us just won't get into God's kingdom! Jesus said as much. He was talking about the day of judgment, and He said, " 'Not everyone who says to Me, "Lord, Lord," shall enter the kingdom of heaven, but he who does the will of My Father in heaven. Many will say to Me in that day, "Lord, Lord, have we not prophesied in Your name, cast out demons in Your name, and done many wonders in Your name?" And then I will declare to them, "I never knew you; depart from Me, you who practice lawlessness" ' " (Matthew 7:21–23).

Evidently, Heaven values obedience more than activity. More than prophesying. More than casting out demons. More than miracles!

*P*lease Pray for Me

A pastor friend of mine once told me about a problem he had faced—a member of his church named Jack, who had become a real sore spot in the congregation. Jack seemed to thrive on dishing out criticism, and he directed most of his barbs at the pastor. Finally, Jack wrote the pastor a long, angry letter listing all his complaints.

The pastor read it and was shocked by the list of accusations against him. He knew he had a good answer for each of them. He knew he could shove these half-truths right back at Jack himself.

But my pastor friend began to pray. And he decided to respond quite differently. He answered Jack with a very short letter containing only four words—"Please pray for me." That was his only reply to Jack's long list of heated accusations.

But those four words stopped all the criticism, cooled all the anger—and the two men, amazingly enough, became good friends.

"Please pray for me." How refreshing those four little words are! How wonderful it would be if that attitude characterized all of us!

ℋ Matter of Priorities

A certain Mr. Coleman was driving to work one day when a woman swerved too close and scraped his fender. Both cars stopped. The young woman looked over the damage and broke into tears. She admitted the accident was her fault, but her car was new—less than two days out of the showroom. How was she ever going to explain this to her husband?

Mr. Coleman was sympathetic, but he also pointed out that they had better exchange license and insurance information. Very reluctantly, the woman reached into her glove compartment. The first paper to tumble out contained a message in a heavy masculine scrawl. She read these words: "In case of accident, remember, honey—it's you I love, not the car."

The more we realize how God has lavished His grace on us, the more we will be able to express that love to others. Extending God's graciousness to others will bring any relationship to life.

𝒯he Same Today and Forever

An author liked to visit an old violin teacher whose homely wisdom was refreshing. He found the teacher one morning sitting in the little room where he taught, and the author said to him by way of greeting, "Well, what is the good news today?"

The old man put down his violin and stepped over to a tuning fork suspended from a silk cord. He struck it a smart blow with a padded mallet and said, "There is the good news for today. That, my friend, is A. It was A all day yesterday. It will be A all day tomorrow, next week, and for a thousand years. The soprano upstairs warbles off-key. The tenor next door flats his high notes. And the piano across the hall is out of tune. Noise all around me. Noise! But that, my friend, is A!"

What if we lived in a world where sunrise was at seven o'clock one morning and at ten o'clock the next? What if an apple tree sometimes grew strawberries and sometimes papayas? What if gravity should come unglued and send us flying off into space? What if the orbits of the stars were so erratic that we must fear collision with some heavenly body at any moment? What if our little planet should wander too near the sun and burn us all up? Who taught nature to be so dependable?

Our God is the same today, yesterday, and forever. We can depend on Him—not only for the physical laws that govern our universe and allow us to life safely but for the spiritual laws that give us life in Him—eternal life.

The Cranes of Ibycus

In the sixth century before Christ—according to an ancient fable—the Greek poet Ibycus was on his way to the music festival at Corinth when he was attacked by two robbers and killed. As he was dying, he saw a flock of cranes flying overhead and called upon them to avenge his death. The robbers heard him.

All Greece was shocked by the violent death of their beloved Ibycus, and the people urged the authorities to bring the offenders to punishment. But this seemed impossible, for there had been no witnesses to the crime.

A few days later, in Corinth, in a theater open to the sky, a huge audience sat spellbound. It so happened that the choristers were impersonating the Furies, as they were called—the goddesses of vengeance. Such a performance, considering the angry mood of the people following Ibycus's death, seemed uncannily appropriate. No one was aware that in the theater, on the top benches, sat the two murderers.

In solemn step the singers slowly advanced. They were clad in black robes and carried blazing torches. Their cheeks were pale as death, and in place of hair, they wore crowns of writhing serpents. Their weird song of vengeance rose higher and higher until it paralyzed the hearts and chilled the blood of the hearers.

At that very moment a flock of cranes swept across the sky and swooped low over the theater. Instantly, from the top benches, there was a cry of terror. "Look, comrade! Look! Yonder are the cranes of Ibycus!"

Every eye turned in the direction of that guilty cry. The murderers had informed against themselves. The atmosphere of vengeance in the theater and the sudden appearance of the ill-omened cranes had been too much for them.

And so the "cranes of Ibycus" have become synonymous with the truth that guilt will not remain hidden; the truth will win out.

Who of us does not identify in some way with this fable? Who of us, at some time, surprised by our personal cranes of Ibycus, has not cried out in the darkened theater of the mind, "I am guilty!"

But, thank God, there is an answer to our guilt. "If we confess our sins, He [Jesus] is faithful and just to forgive us our sins and to cleanse us from all unrighteousness" (1 John 1:9).

Just Empty Space?

Back in the early days of the space race when the Soviet Union was launching satellites and sending cosmonauts into space, the Russian astronauts reported that they had taken a look while spinning around the globe and hadn't found God anywhere. Not even any angels. Just empty space!

What did they expect God to do? Catch their little space ship and take them home to dinner and a tour of heaven?

About this time, an interesting little story circulated among Russian Christians. They said that one day the people in the Kremlin sent up a satellite, and it didn't come back. The Russian leaders were worried. So, they sent an official delegation to the pearly gates and said to Saint Peter, "Sir, we don't want to come in. But, please, may we have our ball back?"

Many a person has been outspoken in expressing doubt. And yet, when something goes wrong and he gets in trouble and doesn't know where to turn, he doesn't hesitate to ask the God he says doesn't exist to give him back his ball. Strange, isn't it?

The Answer to Fear

One day the Perry family was surprised to see some former neighbors—a Los Angeles policeman and his family—attending their church. They had moved from the neighborhood some time before, but here they were—at church!

The policeman said to Mr. Perry, "I know you're wondering why we're here." And then he explained. "You remember the fires four years ago? Brush fires all through the hills—some pretty close. People near the fires evacuated. All the neighbors were in panic—all except your family. We noticed that the Perrys just went to bed and slept. So for four years we've been wanting to come to your church. We wanted to see what kind of religion could let you sleep when the rest of us couldn't!"

Confidence in God's care. Confidence in His love. Confidence that He has everything under control. And the knowledge that your relationship with Him is in working order. That's the answer to fear!

No Weak Links

A story out of the Middle Ages tells of a blacksmith who took great pride in his work. He placed a distinguishing mark on everything that came from his shop, for he wanted people to recognize his unusual skill at the forge.

His country went to war, and the city in which he lived was conquered. The blacksmith was captured and placed in chains. This did not greatly concern him, for he knew all about chains. He knew that in nearly every chain there was one weak link. He planned that when night came, he would find that weak link and break the chain.

That night, in the darkness, his fingers moved confidently along the chain, feeling for the weak link. And then he felt a mark upon one of the links. It was his own mark! His confidence turned to despair, for he knew that there were no weak links in his chains. He had done his work so carefully, made his chains so strong, that now he was hopelessly trapped by the strength of that which he himself had forged!

We search frantically for a weak link that will yield to our wisdom, our technology. There is no question about our skill at the forge. We have proven our ability to make chains. But our hearts have not kept up with our technology. In our saner moments, we realize that our hearts need attention. That we need a Power greater than our own to break out of our self-made prison.

Talking to the Wall

A small boy, admitted to a hospital for some minor surgery, was placed in a room where an intercom made it possible for nurse and patient to talk to each other without the nurse having to leave the nurses' station.

After Bobby was awake from the anesthetic, the nurse called his room and asked, "Bobby, how are you feeling?"

There was no answer. Again, "Bobby, are you all right? How are you feeling?" Still there was no answer. The third time the nurse was more insistent, "Bobby, answer me. How are you feeling?"

Back came a small, timid voice, "I'm all right, wall."

Too many people today are talking to the wall. The trouble is that nobody seems to care. The more sophisticated our technology, the more impersonal our society becomes. Is it any wonder there are so many lonely people? So many hopeless people?

But there is Someone who can heal your loneliness. Someone who cares. You belong to Someone. Jesus can heal your loneliness because He Himself, on a cross outside Jerusalem, endured the keenest, deepest sense of loneliness and separation ever experienced.

Crossing Forty-Second Street

There is a quaint little story about a cat at the corner of Broadway and Forty-Second Street in New York City. And if you've ever been in New

York, you know that's one of the busiest intersections in the world.

Pedestrians were waiting to cross, waiting for the light to change. And a cat came along the sidewalk, up to the curb. She was holding a kitten in her mouth by the back of its neck, as cats do. She wanted to cross the street, but the roar of traffic confused her. Twice she started to cross, but turned back. It was too dangerous.

Then something happened. The traffic officer saw the cat's predicament. Immediately, he put up his hand to stop traffic. He didn't know which way the cat wanted to go, so he stopped traffic going both ways.

Now you understand, of course, that when a traffic officer puts up his hand, it isn't exactly a suggestion or a request. All the authority of the city of New York was behind that lifted hand. The traffic stood still and waited. The cat watched, saw her chance, and darted across the street safely. She never knew that she had been the object of special concern. She never knew that the authority of that great city had been exercised to protect her!

Neither do we know how often strong hands go up to let us pass through some crisis safely. We aren't aware of how often angel hands have been ordered to protect us. We never know that straight from the throne of God has come an order to stop the traffic and clear the way so that God's plan for us may not be hindered!

*L*iberation Day

One August day in 1944, Sergeant Milt Shenton learned that he was going to be the "point man" leading the Fourth Division of the U.S. Army into Paris. That meant he would become the first tempting target the German defenders of the city would sight.

Sergeant Shenton had had the same job on June 6, D-Day, when he led his division across Utah Beach. Amazingly, he'd survived unscathed. But Shenton figured that was all the luck any one man had a right to in a lifetime.

Muttering to himself, Shenton strapped an extra canister of ammunition to his jeep and headed down the empty, menacing street into Paris.

Suddenly a window creaked open. The sergeant whirled around and pointed his carbine.

Then another window opened, and another. From somewhere he heard a woman's voice call out, *"Les Américains!"* Two women in bathrobes, their slippers flopping on the pavement, bolted for the jeep. Suddenly a man was beside Shenton, embracing him and kissing him on both cheeks.

Within seconds a horde of happy, shouting Parisians rushed out of the buildings and filled the street. The soldier who'd felt so alone and vulnerable a moment before was overwhelmed by a sea of exulting, tearful faces.

This was liberation, the day Paris had waited for through the long night of Nazi occupation. Finally, they were free! No more German soldiers patrolling their streets. No more Gestapo beatings. No more Jews deported to death camps. No more resistance fighters lined up and shot. The years of frustration and fear and hunger had ended, this day, this moment.

Everywhere in the city it was the same—deliriously happy crowds rushed on the advancing American and French columns. Jeep drivers were crushed by the people eager to kiss them, touch them, talk to them. Hordes of children clung to tanks and armored cars like bunches of grapes. From sidewalks, people tossed flowers, carrots, radishes—anything they could offer.

They all wanted in some way to make this moment of liberation real. The years of occupation had seemed eternal; Hitler's power had seemed insurmountable at times. It was hard to believe that it was all over, that now they were really free again.

For many GIs these hours would be the most memorable of their lives. Little things stood out: an old French veteran with a handlebar mustache, a row of medals on his faded uniform, standing ramrod straight as the tanks rolled by, great tears coursing down his face. A grandmother lying on a stretcher on the sidewalk, watching the liberators arrive through a mirror held over her head, repeating to the blue skies, "Paris is free; Paris is free."

There were unforgettable reunions that day. An American truck driver watched a woman run through a burst of gunfire and fall on an advancing French infantryman sobbing, "My son, my son."

A French corporal passed handwritten messages to the crowd from his tank, asking for his brother. He'd received no word from him in three years. In the heart of Paris the corporal suddenly noticed a figure making his way slowly down the line of tanks behind him. He stopped his tank and stared in disbelief. There, incredibly thin, in a policeman's uniform much too big for him, wearing a resistance armband, was his long-lost brother. The two men, who symbolized the two halves of fighting France, fell into each other's arms as if pushed by an electric current.

Together at last. Free at last.

The kingdom of the Lord Jesus is going to burst into view someday soon just as surely as those jeeps and tanks rolled into Paris. It's going to be a great day—the Liberation Day for planet Earth. We've been in this long night of frustration and fear for so long. We're been so long under the occupation of the enemy. Sometimes it's hard to believe liberation can be real.

But it's coming! The King is coming! And He's going to wipe away every tear. He's going to wipe out fear. No more starving children with sad eyes and emaciated limbs. No more families torn apart. No more unending heartache for a missing loved one.

Oh, there will be exultation on that day! Delirious joy. There will be shouting and singing and tears of joy. We will be free at last.

I Don't Need to Know

Charlie Shedd was traveling by train with his six-year-old daughter, Karen. A little four-year-old came down the aisle and made friends with Karen. She said her name was Annie Lou, and she was going to a friend's house.

Charlie Shedd asked, "And where does your friend live?"

Annie Lou said, "I really don't know."

"Oh, but aren't you afraid? If you don't know where your friend lives, how will you know when to get off the train and where to go?"

Annie Lou just smiled her million-dollar smile and replied, "Well, you see, I really don't need to know all those things because I'm traveling with my grandmother, and she knows."

We're traveling with our Lord. And He knows the future. We don't need to know.

Going the Wrong Way

You may have heard of an amusing incident that came out of the transportation strike in New York City a few years ago. Certain heavily traveled streets, one of them Madison Avenue, were made one-way. A man who was not completely in possession of all his faculties got onto Madison Avenue going the wrong way.

An officer stopped him and inquired, "Where are you going?"

"I don't know," the man replied. "But I must be late, because everybody's coming back."

Spiritually, the same type of thing can happen. The Bible says, "There is a way that seems right to a man, / But its end is the way of death" (Proverbs 16:25).

When the Fog Lifts

One of the most significant battles in world history was the Battle of Waterloo between the Duke of Wellington and Napoleon Bonaparte. The old priest of Winchester Cathedral never tired of telling the story of the day when news of the battle reached England. It came by sailing vessel to the south coast and was carried overland by semaphore to the top of Winchester Cathedral and then on to London.

The populace eagerly waited as the semaphore spelled out the words, "W-E-L-L-I-N-G-T-O-N D-E-F-E-A-T-E-D—"

Just then a dense fog settled down, and the incomplete message was passed on to London. A pall of gloom and discouragement settled over the land. Streets were barricaded. The people prepared to defend their country in the streets and fields if necessary. But finally the fog lifted, and the semaphore signals began coming through once more: "W-E-L-L-I-N-G-T-O-N D-E-F-E-A-T-E-D T-H-E E-N-E-M-Y."

Can you imagine the wild delirium of joy that spread like a prairie fire, made all the more exhilarating in contrast to the earlier news so grossly misunderstood?

Need I draw the parallel? Does not this experience illustrate the meaning that the disciples read into Christ's crucifixion? The sun refused to shine on the scene. Darkness surrounded the cross and settled over Jerusalem. Resounding peals of thunder reduced the slender faith of the disciples to just two words: "J-E-S-U-S D-E-F-E-A-T-E-D—"

As they laid His limp, lifeless body in a borrowed tomb, their depression deepened. Hear them reasoning, " 'We were hoping that it was He who was going to redeem Israel' " (Luke 24:21). They thought they had made a mistake. Surely Jesus must not be the long-awaited Savior after all.

But then as the light broke on Resurrection morning, the message that should have been understood by His closest followers began to come through more clearly. The world has ever since been able to read the life-giving, glorious message: "J-E-S-U-S D-E-F-E-A-T-E-D D-E-A-T-H."

Appointment in Samarra

The legend says that it happened in the ancient city of Baghdad.

A merchant sent his servant to the market. But soon the servant returned, trembling and greatly agitated, and said to his master, "Down in the marketplace I was jostled by a woman in the crowd, and when I turned around, I saw that it was Death that had jostled me. She looked at me and made a threatening gesture. Master, please lend me your horse, for I must hasten away to avoid her. I will ride to Samarra, and there I will hide, and Death will not find me."

The merchant lent his horse, and the servant galloped away.

About an hour or so later the merchant himself went to the marketplace and saw Death standing in the crowd. He said to her, "Why did you frighten my servant this morning? Why did you make a threatening gesture toward him?"

"That was not a threatening gesture," replied Death. "It was only a start of surprise. I was astonished to see him in Baghdad, for I have an appointment with him tonight in Samarra!"

Only a legend from Baghdad. But it paints a graphic picture of the fatalism that grips countless minds today. Millions of frustrated individuals have decided that this weary planet, with everyone on it, has an appointment with the death angel—its wings bathed in atomic power and propelling us swiftly to oblivion. And they say there is no way to avoid it.

But the Bible is clear that our world will not end in nuclear annihilation or environmental or economic collapse. The Lord Jesus Christ Himself has promised to come back to our planet and rescue His people. He is coming back in splendor and power and glory with all the holy angels with him. He's coming back for you!

When the Rope Breaks

An old legend tells of a Portuguese monastery that stood precariously atop a three-hundred-foot cliff. Visitors were strapped in a huge wicker basket, then pulled to the top by an old ragged rope. As one visitor stepped into the basket for the descent, he asked anxiously, "How often do you get a new rope?"

"Whenever the old one breaks," a monk calmly replied.

We're all like the visitor in the basket. Life is risky, dangerous. We're all hurtling through life on a threadbare rope—ready to break! Everybody knows, of course, that someday the rope *will* break. After all, it does—sometime—for everyone. But the question is this: does it have to break so soon?

For those who have accepted the salvation offered by the Savior, it isn't so important when the earthly life may come to a close. Eternal life lies ahead. Life forever with Jesus and our loved ones. Life that will never end.

Prayer and Miracles

A small boy, with his erector set, was building a mysterious machine that bristled with springs and gears. This was to be no ordinary machine, he told his little sister. It would actually create life.

Unfortunately, she asked him how it worked. He wasn't prepared for that. But then he thought of an answer. He told her that he was depending on prayer—that he would pray hard, and God would work a miracle.

"Then what are all the gears for?" she demanded.

I Will Return!

It happened in the Philippines. General Douglas MacArthur had decided that in order to gain victory, he must delay direct action. Under cover of darkness, accompanied by just a few close aides, he left; but first he promised, "I will return." The end of that story is one of the most dramatic episodes of World War II.

May I take you back to that glad day at the close of the second world conflict when two thousand prisoners of war were delivered from enemy hands? Two of the prisoners had built a little radio and secretly listened to the news. One day they heard a familiar voice, "This is General MacArthur speaking. I have returned!"

What marvelous news! The months had dragged wearily into two and a half long years since the day the general left behind him the promise to return. Now he was returning amid a thunder of guns, with an armada of ships and an air force such as had never before been seen in the Pacific.

In the meantime, the news filtered through the camp that the enemy, sensing the hopelessness of its own situation, had actually decreed the death of the prisoners.

Among the prisoners was one who had been asked to serve as a camp official. One evening the guard informed him that at seven o'clock the next morning he was to call the prisoners together. Could this be the time when they would hear the long-feared death sentence?

Frightful were those hours as the camp official watched the hands of the clock moving toward the decisive moment. Then he went out with the bell ringer to call the camp. The steel bar was raised, ready to strike the gong.

Suddenly both men looked up. In unison they exclaimed, "Look! Planes!"

The bell ringer, his hand still in the air, watched in breathless anticipation. Nearer and nearer they came. They roared overhead. Paratroopers leaped out into the prison yards. Deliverance at last!

Make no mistake about it. The forces of evil are intent on destroying the human race. The enemy of God has his hand raised, ready to strike the death gong. The great controversy between Christ and Satan, between good and evil, is on the verge of its last titanic struggle. But it is written in the Bible: " 'At that time your people shall be delivered' " (Daniel 12:1). At that time—look up! Deliverance is near!

Struck by Lightning

The flight of *Apollo 12* was normal for thirty-six seconds. Suddenly lightning struck the spacecraft. The master alarm sounded, and lights flashed on all over the control panel. Said Dick Gordon later: "In all our training, we had never seen so many alarm lights as went on inside that spacecraft. . . . If they had given us something like that in the simulators, we would have said, 'What are you trying to do? This is impossible!' "

The best thing to do at the moment was nothing. But once in orbit, everything depended on getting the inertial guidance system back in shape.

Dick Gordon crawled down into the equipment bay and tried to sight some stars in order to realign the guidance platform. But as he looked through the telescope, he couldn't see a single star. He actually wondered, for a moment, if the stars had gone out. Then, as his eyes adapted to the dark, he caught just the bottom of the constellation Orion. He sighted on Rigel, then Sirius. *Apollo 12* was back in business.

We, too, are aboard a spacecraft struck by lightning. We are hurtling through space at sixty-seven thousand miles an hour, with our guidance system badly out of adjustment. Every alarm in the capsule is flashing. It could be our last chance, say many thinking men.

But while we cannot depend on this earth for survival, we can depend on the One who created our world and everything in it. He has said, "I will be with you. I will not leave you or forsake you. Don't be afraid" (see Deuteronomy 31:8).

A Mother's Love

I think of the Australian lumberman who built a little cabin at the edge of the woods. One evening as he returned from work, a horrible scene met his sight. A forest fire had swept through and destroyed his little home. Only a smoking heap remained.

He wandered out to where the old chicken coop had stood. It, too, was a mass of ashes and burned wire. At his feet lay a mound of charred feathers. He idly kicked it over. And what do you suppose happened? Four little fuzzy babies scrambled out. Four little chicks survived, sheltered by their mother's love.

Friend, do you want to be covered when fire sweeps through this planet? You can be. You can be sheltered in your Savior now.

Two Paces Forward

However inadequate illustrations may be, I shall never forget the surge of loyal dedication that rose up in my heart for the Lord Jesus Christ as I first heard of an event that took place during one of the most decisive battles in the history of the British Empire.

The Duke of Wellington had planned an operation to take a dangerous hill. That famous general knew that when he gave the command for his men to charge, very few would come back alive. Even his stout military heart wavered at the thought. He told his regiments, "I will turn about, and every man who is willing at daybreak to make the charge on that hill, let him take two paces forward."

The general turned and waited. In a few moments an officer asked him to turn again. A look of disappointment momentarily crossed his face, for there was not a break in the lines. Yes, a look of disappointment momentarily—until the officer explained, "Every man has taken two paces forward!"

What else can a man do when he faces the claims of the Lord Jesus Christ? What else can he do but step forward? It is a matter of loyalty!

How Does the Bee Know?

A little honeybee has discovered a field of flowers and is ready to return to the hive with a sample of the nectar and pollen. How will it find its way back? Keep in mind that it may be several miles from the hive and that its search for nectar may have led it in several directions before it made its discovery. Yet, it will fly straight back to the hive!

Who told the bee how to do it? What sort of navigational equipment does it possess? And once back in the hive, how will it communicate to its thousands of fellow bees the location of the treasure it has found?

It is true that bees are able to distinguish odors with great skill. If a bee returns to the hive with nectar from flowers nearby, the other bees will leave the hive and fly directly to the source. And they also act as if they have an internal clock. If they discover that food is available at a particular time of day, they return for more at the same hour the next day.

But what if the flowers are several miles distant? Surely there must be some limitation to the tiny creatures' sense of smell. What then? How can the little bee get across to its fellow bees the location of the treasure?

Well, you haven't heard anything yet. Let me tell you about the "waggle dance"!

Sometimes a bee that returns with nectar and pollen goes through a peculiar performance that many scientists believe is its way of communicating the location of the source of nectar. It gives samples of the nectar to the other bees and gets them all excited. Then, as they watch, it does a fancy dance before them—called the waggle dance because of the way the bee waggles its abdomen. It goes through a figure eight across the face of the comb. And the astonishing thing is that the angle of the dance down the vertical comb seems to represent the horizontal direction of the food source with respect to the direction of the sun.

And not only that. The number of dances per minute indicates the distance to the field. But surprisingly, the number is in reverse ratio to the distance! That is, the farther away the field, the smaller the number. In other words, if the bee goes through ten rounds in fifteen seconds, the field of flowers is three hundred feet away. But if the bee moves in slow motion, say two rounds in fifteen seconds, the flowers are almost four miles away. And listen to this. A little calculation will show that this relationship to distance is not one of simple arithmetic, but is logarithmic! What do you think of that?

What kind of brain does the little honeybee have? Who taught it to do all this? How did this tiny creature learn to relate sun angles and distances to dance-step routines? And how is it that millions of bees understand the language?

Now, I'm aware that some scientists are not convinced that bees *do* understand the language. They aren't convinced that this strange dance really does communicate to other bees the location of a field of flowers. I'm aware of the controversy over this matter.

But if, by any chance, you are inclined to doubt, then consider this. A bee, by means of this dance, can communicate the location to human beings. Humans can understand it. Humans can watch the dance and find the field of flowers. Is that any less striking? Is it any less a miracle to communicate that information to human beings, in logarithmic terms, than to get it across to other bees? I think not!

What kind of brain does the little honeybee have? Is it an accident?

No, my friend, it is no accident. The honeybee and its amazing abilities come from the mind and heart of God—the same God who designed you and me and who has sent His Son to be our Savior. Don't you think we can trust Him to care for us just as He has cared for the needs of the little honeybee?

Refusing to Heed the Warning

Just a regular mountain, it seemed. Tall, but not so spectacular as some of its Cascade neighbors. Then one May morning in 1980, Mount St. Helens shuddered awake and blew its top! That volcano belched forth plumes of steam and ash thousands of feet into the sky—an explosion comparable to Vesuvius burying Pompeii.

Almost a hundred miles downwind in Yakima, Washington, the sun went out at noon, leaving the city in total blackness for several hours. The ash lay ankle deep, as it was in much of eastern Washington.

Those who lived around Mount St. Helens had heard the warnings of an imminent eruption. Some listened and escaped. Others delayed. . . .

I think of eighty-four-year-old Harry Truman—not the former president but the owner of the Mount St. Helens Lodge at the edge of Spirit Lake. He had lived safely by the mountain for more than half a century. Nobody was going to tell him what to do. "After all," he boasted, "no one knows more about this mountain than Harry, and it doesn't dare blow up on me."

But it did. The overwhelming surprise came with a shattering blast that blew a cubic mile of material into the sky. Poor Harry Truman and dozens of others lay buried beneath tons of volcanic silt. They gambled their lives and lost. They had been warned, but they refused to be saved.

Why do we find it so hard to heed warnings?

If you have never accepted Jesus' offer of forgiveness and eternal life, perhaps He is asking you to make that decision right now. There will never be a better time. Just tell Him that you know you are a sinner; tell Him that you believe He came to earth to be your Savior and that He died for your sins on the cross; then tell Him that you accept the forgiveness He has promised.

What Is Man?

Mark Twain, in his story "Captain Stormfield's Visit to Heaven," shared a tale that was obviously intended to be completely absurd. Captain Stormfield, the story goes, had died and was on his way to heaven but was unable to resist the temptation to race with a comet. He ended up way off course in a sort of heavenly "missing persons bureau." An angel, wanting to help, went up in a balloon alongside a huge map of the universe, hoping to locate our solar system. The map was about the size of the whole state of Rhode Island. Three days later the angel came back down to report that he might have found our solar system, but he couldn't be sure. It might have been just flyspecks!

Just an absurd piece of exaggeration. Never intended to be taken seriously. But we know now that Mark Twain may not have been so far off. We are like a tiny cinder on the edge of the universe. Could the Creator ever be concerned with us? Does He even know that we are here?

It was David who wrote, "When I consider Your heavens, the work of Your fingers, / The moon and the stars, which You have ordained, / What is man that You are mindful of him, / And the son of man that You visit him?" (Psalm 8:3, 4).

The Story of the Hands

You may have heard the story of the unbeliever who rescued an orphan boy from a burning building. Having lost his own wife and child, he wanted to adopt the lad. Christian neighbors were skeptical about the wisdom of placing the boy in an infidel home. But the applicant won his case when he held up his hands, badly burned in rescuing the lad from the fire, and said, "I have only one argument. It is these hands."

He proved to be a good father, and little Jimmy never tired of hearing how Daddy had saved him from the fire. And he liked best to hear about the scarred hands. One day with his new father he visited a display of art masterpieces. One painting interested him especially. It pictured Jesus reproving Thomas for his unbelief and holding out His scarred hands.

"Tell me the story of that picture, Daddy," the little fellow begged.

"No, not that one."

"Why not?"

"Because I don't believe it."

"But you tell me the story of Jack and the beanstalk, and you don't believe that either."

So, the man told his son the story. And Jimmy said, "It's like you and me, Daddy." And then he went on, "It wasn't nice of Thomas to not believe after the good Man had died for him. What if they had told me how you saved me from the fire and I had said I didn't believe you did it?"

The father couldn't escape the sound reasoning of a small child. He had used his own scarred hands to win a small boy's heart. Could he continue to resist the scarred hands of the Man who had died for him—and say He didn't do it? The mightiest argument of all is the cross of Calvary. The scarred hands of Jesus. Hands that were wounded in His encounter with the forces of evil—so that you and I could live! What can we do but fall at His feet and say with Thomas, " 'My Lord and my God!' " (John 20:28).

In the Beginning

Christmas Eve 1968 was a bright spot in an otherwise very turbulent year. A beacon of hope came to us that night, the thrill of accomplishment. For the first time in history, human beings were in outer space, orbiting the moon. And they were Americans! We could hardly believe our eyes as television relayed the dramatic lunar vista beneath *Apollo 8.* Astronauts Frank Borman, James Lovell, and William Anders sent their Christmas greetings from a quarter million miles away. Then they read to us the first chapter of an old Book. Comforting words, somehow familiar and yet nearly forgotten: "In the beginning God created the heavens and the earth."

The New York Times, commenting on that scripture reading from lunar orbit, observed, "Somehow it was exactly right." Yes, what could have been more appropriate for our astronauts than to recognize that the blue sphere they looked back on exists not by accident but because God put it here?

Some months after the mission of *Apollo 8,* I learned of a unusual incident that had taken place that Christmas Eve. Naturally, many reporters were present at the Space Center in Houston, some of them from foreign nations. Among them were two from a country without a Christian background. These men had been deeply impressed as the astronauts read from Genesis. The stark splendor of those grand words touched their minds and hearts.

Not realizing they had been listening to Scripture, they asked someone from NASA if a script of what the astronauts had read might be available. The American official replied with a meaningful smile, "Why, yes, when you get back to your hotel room, just open the drawer of your nightstand. You will find a Book bound in black. And the script from which the astronauts read is on the very first page."

An Ordinary Package

Harry Winston, a famous diamond broker, was excited. And so was the crowd that had gathered around him. He had just purchased one of the most famous diamonds in the world. And he expected it to be delivered at any moment!

In the crowd were friends and news reporters and curious onlookers, all anxious for the first glimpse of the famous stone. While they waited, Mr. Winston entertained them with stories from the diamond's history. The crowd buzzed with excitement.

The people kept watching for the armored car and police escort that would make the delivery. Security was sure to be tight.

At the edge of the crowd a man in a postman's uniform tried to make his way through, but he was shoved back. The people wanted nothing to distract attention from the arrival of the fabled gem.

The crowd grew. Self-appointed sentinels kept their eyes on the roadway, ready to shout the arrival of the armed escort. Again the postman tried to push through the crowd. In his hand he clutched a brown paper parcel tied with string. He said he had to deliver it to Mr. Winston. Imagine! Who was he? Some crackpot trying to get his name in the paper?

Finally, with more irritation than courtesy, they let the stubborn postman through. Mr. Winston took the parcel, glanced at the return address, and gave a short cry. With trembling hands he tore the paper away from a small box. Then he opened it and tenderly lifted the precious diamond for all to see. He held it up to the sun and let the gem's reflections play over the amazed crowd.

For a few moments they stood in stunned silence. How could such fabled beauty arrive in such a common wrapping? And then they burst into a loud, spontaneous cheer!

But no one in that crowd ever forgot how they had almost rejected one of the world's most precious diamonds!

How like what happened nearly two thousand years ago when Jesus came to earth. The people were expecting their Messiah. They were waiting for Him, longing for His arrival, but they didn't think He would come in such a plain, unassuming package.

What Makes the Difference?

It will take all eternity to really understand what Calvary cost. And yet, just as with any gift, we begin to appreciate it only as we begin to realize its value.

Let me illustrate. Suppose that I am visiting you in your home. As we talk, I notice a lovely vase there on the coffee table. I pick it up and admire it. And suddenly—I don't know how it happens—it slips from my hand and onto the floor and breaks!

I say, "Oh, I'm so sorry." I apologize again and again. And of course I offer to pay for it. I reach for my wallet. I know I have a twenty-dollar bill, so I think I'm safe.

But you tell me more about the vase and how you happen to have it. You tell me that there are only two of these in the world. The other one is in a museum in New York City. And it's valued at fifty thousand dollars!

Am I any sorrier now than I was a few moments ago? Yes. I am fifty thousand dollars sorrier! What made the difference? Knowing the cost. Knowing the cost made the difference.

Do you see?

It is only as we look long and earnestly at the cross of Calvary—only as we realize who it was who died there—it is only then that we begin to realize what our forgiveness cost. It is only as we see the most valuable life ever lived, the loveliest character ever seen by human beings—it is only as we see that life broken there on the cross by our own hands—it is only then that we begin to appreciate the value of the salvation made possible that day, the gift that is now ours for the asking!

It would be unthinkable that we should reject it!

Only One Night!

A number of years ago a man named Luther Warren, a mighty preacher of God, was invited to speak for a series of nightly meetings in Jamaica. A large hall was rented in the city of Kingston, and young ministers for miles around came to watch this man in action.

On the first night, the hall was crowded. The young ministers were there in the front seats. Luther Warren stepped into the pulpit. But something strange happened. In a few minutes, the preacher had covered his announced subject and turned to another. Then another. He had left introductory truth behind and had turned to the most vital challenges that can claim a person's attention.

He talked of obedience. He talked of judgment. He talked of decision. As those who had sponsored the meetings watched in amazement from the rear of the auditorium, Luther Warren invited men and women to come forward to the altar in complete commitment to Christ and His truth for this last hour. And the people surged forward under the power of deep conviction.

Why had he preached as he did—combining all the subjects he had planned to cover over several days into a single evening's sermon? Why had he touched every challenging truth in a single night? No one knew. Luther Warren himself did not know.

But the next morning it was crystal clear. For a large part of Kingston lay in ruins at the hand of a great earthquake. For many of those who had listened to Luther Warren the previous evening, there had been only one night!

I ask you, isn't is just like God to send a last warning message to men and women facing peril?

Anywhere He Leads

We can learn so much from children. A friend of mine has a little boy named Stevie who loves to go places with him. Anyplace at all, it matters not where, just so long as he can be with Daddy. Whenever Stevie sees his father heading for the door, car keys in hand, he pleads, "May I go with you?" Only after they start on their way does he ask, "Daddy, where are we going?"

Are we willing to trust our heavenly Father and go anywhere He leads?

Blind Spots

Karl Marx wrote passionately about the poor, especially the working-class poor. His *Communist Manifesto* is a famous battle cry for the down-trodden masses to rise up and seize power from their rich oppressors. Although he lived a very conventional, middle-class life in nineteenth-century England, Marx worked tirelessly for revolutionary change. An intense moral vision of justice for impoverished people dominated his life.

But there was one impoverished person he seemed incapable of really seeing. For many years, Helene Demuth worked faithfully as a servant for the Marx family. But one day Karl Marx either raped or seduced her, and she became pregnant. Karl's wife didn't find out about this until the child was born. It was a son, named Frederich Demuth.

Karl Marx had only daughters and badly wanted a son. But he denied any connection with Frederich. The boy grew up without a father. Karl Marx would have nothing to do with him. He was busy creating the legend of a revolutionary hero—the rape of a servant girl just wouldn't fit.

Karl Marx saw so clearly the desperate conditions of the impoverished workers of England. But he couldn't see the needs of the poor girl he had wronged or the son he rejected.

Blind spots. They plague us all. The great moral duties to humanity are clear to us, but specific obligations to our neighbors grow hazy. The faults that stand out so sharply in others are all but invisible to ourselves.

Rules and Hearts

A friend of mine shared a personal experience that helps me understand what it means to disobey God.

As a boy, my friend attended a little country school—thirteen students in eight grades in one room. The teacher was a seventeen-year-old girl, fresh out of school. As you can imagine, she had her hands full keeping law and order. Soon her struggle to maintain discipline became a losing battle.

One afternoon outside the schoolhouse, my friend joined his peers in complaining about classes. He voiced his dislike for the teacher. How much he hated her rules. How much he wished she would go away.

Just then he happened to glance through the open window. There stood that poor teacher, her shoulders quivering with sobs. The sight of her sorrow pierced him like a sword. He realized now that misbehavior meant more than breaking a rule. He had broken a heart. Overwhelmed with remorse and repentance, he determined to become a new boy. And he did!

This is the realization we need. We need to learn that indulging in sin means more than merely breaking God's law. It also breaks His heart.

What a Sermon!

Seven men worked side by side in the blazing sun, hoeing long rows across a huge plot of land. The boss would return at evening to inspect their work.

At noon the men exchanged their hoes for lunch pails and found a piece of shade. As the others began eating, one—a gray-haired man they called Old Lew—dropped to one knee and bowed his head. They were used to this ritual and paid no attention.

All too soon the half hour allotted for lunch was over, and Old Lew rose to go back to work.

"Sit down, Lew. It's too hot to be hurrying out there," said Dan. "The boss'll never know the difference if we take an extra fifteen minutes."

"You men do what you want," Old Lew replied as he stepped out into the sun.

When he had gone, Dan shook his head. "I don't get it. What difference would a few extra minutes make anyhow?"

"To him, plenty. An honest day's work is part of his religion, part of him." It was Young Lew who had spoken up. They called him "Young Lew" to distinguish him from the older man.

And now it was Dan again. "Look, you don't have to stick up for him just because you're courting his daughter. The way I look at it, we work because we have to. So if you can go easy on yourself, who does it hurt?"

"It would hurt him," Young Lew tried to explain. "The agreement was for a half-hour lunch."

"I don't trust him and that crazy religion of his," countered Dan.

Bill disagreed. "He's OK, he don't bother nobody."

And now Rube spoke up. "I admire him. If only he didn't have that funny religion."

And Young Lew said, "Wait a minute. What makes him the man you admire *is* his religion. You can't have it both ways."

Maybe it was to ease this tension that Tom Wilson came up with a joke he'd heard the night before. That reminded Bill of one, and then Rube told his favorite. The time was forgotten.

Suddenly Rube shouted, "Hey! Look at the time!"

The men leaped to their feet and began running toward the field. "That old man will be across the field and back," Dan shouted.

"The boss will know we've been goofing off," called another.

"The old man will probably tell him." That was from Dan.

But Young Lew panted, "He won't have to tell. Our rows will tell the story."

They raced on together. In the distance they could see Old Lew, bent over his hoe. Then, as they neared the field, suddenly they stopped. There, just as they had expected, Old Lew's row was a long way ahead of where it had been before lunch. *But the other six rows were all even with his!*

They couldn't believe what they saw. But when they saw the old man step from one row to the next, they knew it was true. He had been stepping from one row to another, keeping each man's row even with his own!

What a sermon! A sermon preached by a man with a hoe! Here was love in action.

What if the love of God for us had been all talk and no action? What if Jesus had not bothered to come and die for us? What if He had wept divine tears over our plight—and sent us messages, eloquent in their sympathy for our fallen condition. But nothing more.

Have you ever thought how dark this world would be if Calvary had never happened?

Following the Crowd

Jean-Henri Fabre, a French naturalist, made a study of processionary caterpillars. It seems that this particular kind of caterpillar wanders about aimlessly, pursued by many followers who move when he moves, stop when he stops, and eat when he eats. Pine needles are their principal source of food.

One day Fabre tried an experiment. He filled a flowerpot with pine needles, which these caterpillars love. Then he lined up the caterpillars in a solid ring around the rim of the pot. Sure enough, they began to move slowly around and around the rim, each following the one ahead. And yes, you guessed it. They continued this senseless march for seven days, never once stopping for food—until one by one they began to collapse.

No, it's not always safe to follow the crowd. In fact, it is almost *never* safe to do so. Jesus said, " 'Wide is the gate and broad is the way that leads to destruction, and there are many who go in by it. Because narrow is the gate and difficult is the way which leads to life, and there are few who find it' " (Matthew 7:13, 14).

Freedom!

It is said that back in the old days, on the bank of the Mississippi River, Abraham Lincoln stood near a slave market. He watched the tragic sight of families being torn apart. Their heartbreaking sobs pierced his heart. Clenching his fists, he vowed, "If I ever get a chance to hit this thing, I'll hit it hard!" And he did.

Before Lincoln's great emancipation, a slave named Joe was shoved on the auction block. Bitter and resentful, he muttered, "I won't work! I won't work!" But a wealthy landowner purchased him anyway.

He led Joe to the carriage, and they drove out of town to the plantation. There by a lake stood a little bungalow. With curtains, flowers, and a cobblestone walkway. The new master stopped the carriage. Turning to Joe, he smiled. "Here's you new home. You don't have to work for it. I've bought you to set you free."

For a moment Joe sat stunned. Then his eyes filled with tears. Overwhelmed, he exclaimed, "Master, I'll serve you forever!"

One day long ago, Someone from a land far away looked down on this earth. He saw our bondage to Satan and heard our cry for freedom from sin. He determined, "Someday I'll get a chance to hit this thing, and I'll hit it hard." Jesus did just that. By His death He set us free.

Love Is Something We Do

From old England comes the story of a young boy named Bron who went to church for the very first time with his governess. His parents were not Christians, and so Bron had never been to church before. But they decided it would be good for their son to go to hear the preaching and instructed the governess to take him to services the next week.

Sitting in the pew, Bron watched the minister climb high into the pulpit. Then he heard the minister tell a terrible piece of news. He told how an innocent Man had been nailed to a cross and left to die.

How terrible! the lad thought. *How wrong!* Surely the people in church would be upset and do something about it. But he looked about him, and no one seemed concerned. *They must be waiting for church to be over,* he decided. Then surely they would do something to right the terrible deed.

He walked out of church trembling with emotion, with tears in his eyes, waiting to see what the crowd would do. And his governess said, "Bron! Don't take it to heart. Someone will think you are strange."

Strange—to be upset, disturbed by injustice? Strange—to be stirred by so tragic a recital? Strange—to care and want desperately to do something about it?

Love is more than just something we say. Love is something we do.

I'm Guilty!

It happened in the early part of the seventeenth century. The Duke of Osuna, who was viceroy of Sicily, and later of Naples, came aboard a galley ship one day as it lay at anchor in the harbor of Barcelona.

Below deck were criminals who for one crime or another had been sentenced to row at the oars of the galley ship. Some of them would row at the oars until the day of their death.

The duke sat down on the deck of the ship and ordered that these men, one at a time, be brought before him. Of each man he asked the same question, "For what crime are you here?"

They were serving their sentences for various crimes—some for robbery, some for murder, some from treason. But through all their answers ran a common thread. Each man protested his innocence. Each had some excuse. And each blamed somebody else.

Finally a young man only twenty years old was brought on deck. He was so ashamed to be appearing before the duke that he hung his head. "For what crime are you here?" the duke asked.

And the young prisoner replied, "Sir, I wanted some money, and I stole to get it. I was justly tried and convicted. I deserve this punishment."

The duke was so surprised to hear this honest admission of guilt, so happily amazed, that he granted the young man a full and complete pardon. He said to him with a twinkle in his eye, "Young man, you are far too bad to be among all these good and innocent men."

And he set him free!

That young man may not have known it, but he had just taken the first step, often the hardest step, in becoming a Christian. He had admitted his guilt.

It Doesn't Take Long

Paul Tournier, the famous Swiss psychiatrist, in his college days had become quite attached to a professor who had taken an interest in him. Though the professor was not a Christian, he was a kind man.

Many years later Dr. Tournier, long after becoming a Christian, completed his first book manuscript about the Christian life. He wanted someone to read it critically. He thought of his old former professor.

The professor asked Dr. Tournier to read aloud the first chapter of his book, for his eyesight was no longer the best. When the chapter was completed, Dr. Tournier looked to him for some reaction and comment. The professor said, "Paul, read another chapter."

So Tournier read the second chapter. The professor said, "Paul, please continue." And he read the third chapter. Then the aging teacher said, "Paul, we must pray together."

They prayed. And then, still amazed, Dr. Tournier exclaimed, "I didn't know you were a Christian!"

"Oh, yes."

"When did you become a Christian?"

"Just now," the old man answered.

Just now. That's how long it takes to become a Christian. That's how long it takes to make a decision. And that decision can mark the beginning of a new life in Christ.

Obeying or Agreeing?

Bill grew up on a farm. And there was never any question about his future. He would be a farmer like his dad.

He went to college and studied agriculture. That gave him the scientific know-how. But where would he get the money to buy a farm?

One day his father said, "Bill I'm getting old. I'm almost ready to retire. I'd like to give the farm to you."

Bill was speechless. His problem was solved!

But the older man went on. "There's just one stipulation. I want you to run the farm strictly according to my directions for the first year. After that, it's yours."

That was fair enough. Dad was a good farmer. He knew what he was doing. And just think—after a year, the farm would be his!

The two men spent the next few days going from field to field. Bill carried a notebook and wrote down just what his father wanted him to plant in each field. Then his father and mother left for a vacation.

Bill was curious. It would be interesting to see how his father's directions checked out with what he had learned at college. He got out his soil-testing kit and started around the farm again. As he went from one field to another, he was impressed with his father's wisdom. In each field his dad had scooped up a handful of soil and examined it carefully before deciding what to plant. And he had been right every time. Every time he had chosen the very crop that, according to what Bill had learned in college, would grow best in that particular soil.

Every time—until Bill came to the last field. His father had said to plant corn, but he must have made a mistake. The soil appeared to be sandy and poor. Plant corn! Why, Bill was sure that the slightest wind would tear the plants right out of the soil. And even if the stalks weren't blown over, he was sure the corn would be sickly. Dad must have made a mistake.

Bill's analysis showed that the soil would be perfect for peanuts. Dad would want every crop to be a success. He would be pleased to see that all the money spent on Bill's education had paid off. So, Bill planted peanuts.

Dad came back at harvest time. He said the farm had never looked so good. Bill took him around and showed him the wheat and the potatoes and the alfalfa.

"But where's the corn?" Dad wanted to know. "I thought I told you to plant corn."

Bill said, "Well, yes, Dad. That was in this field over here. I went back and tested the soil in all the fields. You were exactly right in all except this one, so I thought you must have made a mistake. I was sure you would rather see a good crop of peanuts than a sickly crop of corn."

Dad shook his head sadly. "Bill," he said, "you haven't followed my directions in any of these fields. You've followed your own judgment in every case. It just happened that you agreed with me in all points except one. But as soon as there was any question, you did what you thought was best in spite of what I had directed you to do. I'm sorry, Bill, but you'll have to look elsewhere for a farm of your own."

How about it? Was Bill's father too harsh? Or was he absolutely right? Does it mean anything at all to follow directions—especially when they are God's directions—only when we happen to agree with them?

Our Father, like Bill's dad, has given us some specific directions. He's written them on slabs of stone—the Ten Commandments. And on condition that we follow them, He promises not a farm but a future beyond our wildest dreams—never-ending life.

But if we obey only when we agree with what God has said, have we obeyed at all? Jesus said, " 'Not everyone who says to Me, "Lord, Lord," shall enter the kingdom of heaven, but he who does the will of My Father in heaven' " (Matthew 7:21).

Guarding Weeds

It is said that a young Russian tsar, many years ago, was walking one day in the royal gardens when he noticed that out in a nearby field a palace guard was standing at attention in all his pomp and ceremony.

Curious, the tsar walked out into the field and asked the young soldier what he was guarding. He didn't know—except that orders called for a sentry to be stationed at this spot.

The young tsar looked up the records. He discovered that at one time Catherine the Great had sponsored acres of rare rose gardens. And on that spot a choice and beautiful rosebush had grown. Every week she permitted the peasants from the surrounding area to come and view the roses. But she ordered a sentry to stand guard over that particular bush. The order had never been rescinded. The rose gardens had long since disappeared. But a sentry still stood guard *over a patch of weeds!*

Things change in this deteriorating world of ours. Roses are replaced with weeds. Wells go dry. And worship, once sincere and fresh, becomes only a hollow form.

Following the Right Shepherd

A boy was herding his father's sheep. Not far away, across a little valley, a neighbor boy was likewise herding sheep for his father. The boys were good friends. They often called to each other across the valley that separated their homes.

One day a severe storm came up very suddenly, and the boys, with their sheep, took refuge under the same huge stone ledge. When the storm was over and it was time to go home, the boys had a problem. They couldn't separate the sheep. Some of them they knew, but they weren't sure about the others.

Finally, in desperation, and fearful that they would be scolded, they started for home—one down one steep path and the other down a path leading to the opposite side of the valley. And what happened? The sheep just separated themselves perfectly, each sheep following his own shepherd!

Today, the sheep are sorting themselves out, each one following his or her own shepherd. By their responses, by their actions, the sheep are separating themselves into two camps—those who go their own way and those who love and follow the Good Shepherd.

No Questions

The story is told of a railway worker who lived near the tracks. He was off duty that day. He looked up from his work in the yard to see his little boy, four and a half years old, playing on the tracks. And a train was thundering toward him!

There was no time to reach Johnny and snatch him away. He called, but Johnny didn't hear. The train was drawing ever closer. Then the father called out at the top of his voice, for there was nothing else he could do, "Johnny, lie down and don't move!"

Johnny heard and obeyed instantly, without even turning to look his father's way. At that instant the train rushed over the motionless boy. And after the caboose had passed, the father gathered up his son, both hearts pounding—but Johnny was safe!

There was nothing in Johnny's short experience, his few short years of life, to qualify him to understand his father's strange command. But he didn't question it. He didn't ask why. He didn't delay. His father had spoken. And that was enough for him.

Our heavenly Father has spoken—and that should be enough.

The Worst Sinner in Town

Samuel Chadwick, a great Methodist preacher, was young and inexperienced—and self-confident—as he began his ministry. He prepared his sermons with the utmost care. He worked hard. But nothing was being accomplished either inside or outside of the little church under his care.

Then God did something for him personally. His own heart was renewed, and his members were revived. During this time, as he read from the Gospel of John, he was intrigued by the story of Jesus raising Lazarus from the dead. He was impressed by the fact that many came to see Lazarus, the man Jesus had called back to life. And when they had seen Lazarus, a living demonstration of the power of Christ, then they were ready to listen to Jesus.

So, Chadwick decided that what his little church needed was a Lazarus—a man so dead and buried in sin that he seemed completely hopeless. And Chadwick, along with his members, began praying that God would save the worst sinner in town.

They prayed for weeks. And then it happened. The man came of his own accord. He was a dreadful character. Everybody in town knew him; nobody ever expected he would be any better. So far as the man himself could remember, he had never been to a religious service except in jail. He was the terror of the neighborhood.

Well, he came to church and signed a temperance pledge. The members wanted to pray with him. But he said, "Not this time. One thing at a time." So they continued to pray. Two weeks later he came to church again, and the members' hearts nearly stood still as they saw this big, rough man in his work clothes walk down the aisle and fling himself on his knees.

The next morning he told his fellow workmen what had happened. And they laughed. In the past they wouldn't have dared to say a cross word to him. But now he was changed. He didn't retaliate. So, they persecuted him cruelly.

One day as they were working, a bar slipped and jammed his finger. Before he was aware of it, a curse word flew from his lips. The men laughed—but only for a moment. They released his finger and wanted to wrap it up, but he wouldn't let them. Tears streamed down his face as he said in a broken voice, "I've a bigger wound than this; we'll have that seen to first."

And then, surrounded by the men who had heard him swear, he dropped to his knees and prayed earnestly and simply for forgiveness. When he had finished, he stood up and said, "It's all right. God has forgiven me. Now we'll have to get the finger wrapped up."

You can guess what happened. The news of his conversion spread like wildfire. Hundreds came to the little church from far and near to see the man Christ had raised from the dead as surely as He had raised Lazarus!

Said Chadwick, "The resurrection of Jesus Christ from the dead is the New Testament standard of power. It is the sample and pledge of what God can do for human beings."

Yes, the resurrection of Jesus is the sample and pledge of what God wants to do—and can do—for you and me.

Master Designer

In the 1850s, architect Sir Joseph Paxton entered a competition to design the building that would house London's Great Exhibition. He longed to outdo his rivals with an epoch-making design. Paxton conjured up a building of gigantic dimensions that would have nothing heavy or clumsy about it; he imagined a structure that would produce the effect of lightness, even weightlessness. But the problem was, there was no way to construct such a building at the time. Large structures required massive walls to support them. There seemed no way to create the graceful, airy building Paxton had in mind.

But then he remembered a certain plant he'd worked with as a gardener—the royal water lily. The floating leaves of this lily are huge, up to six feet in diameter, *and* very thin. But in spite of this, they're quite stable.

They achieve this stability by a complicated strutting on the underside. Ribs radiate from the center of the leaf outward, splitting up into many branches.

The royal water lily gave Paxton the key to making his architectural dream come true. He used a few main struts connected by many small ribs in his design. And he won the competition. The result? The Crystal Palace of the World Exhibition, a magnificent success. It proved to be a great turning point in architecture. The bold skyscrapers of steel and glass we see all around us today actually spring from that graceful, airy Crystal Palace, and yes, from the remarkable design of the royal water lily.

The Bible says that the marvelous things of nature show the evidence of their Creator and can teach us about His power and His love.

A Spectacular Rescue

It was September 23, 1922. The old USS *Mississippi,* with a new owner and a new name, lay at anchor in the harbor of Mytilene—an island in the Aegean Sea. In the gray morning a young American civilian had come out to the ship in a borrowed rowboat and asked to see the captain. And now, twelve hours later, he had just delivered an ultimatum to the Greek government!

It happened this way. Not many weeks earlier the YMCA had sent this civilian—Asa Jennings—with his wife and family to the Turkish city of Smyrna. His assignment—to study what might be done to smooth relations between the Turks and Armenians and Greeks and Jews of that troubled city.

Things had happened fast. The Allies had given Smyrna to the Greeks as a reward for their participation in World War I. The Greek army had moved into Smyrna and pushed inland toward Ankara. But Ataturk had rallied the Turkish people behind him in a daring drive for independence.

The Greek army was confident of victory. Its troops were pushing steadily toward the heart of the country—when suddenly they retreated before Ataturk. They burned and pillaged their way back to Smyrna.

The Greek troops, in their wild retreat, forced their own countrymen, as well as the Armenians, to abandon their homes and flee to the coast. Every road to the sea was choked with refugees. And then, believe it or not, the Greek soldiers, thinking only of their own safety, simply took ship and sailed away. The refugees were left to make out as best they could.

And then suddenly—no one seems to know just how—Smyrna was in flames. The great mass of refugees was pushed toward the sea, with the fire behind them.

Asa Jennings, while the city was still burning, put his little family aboard an American destroyer. But he stayed behind to see what he could do for the refugees. Somehow he arranged for food to be sent in. But this suffering mass of humanity that choked the quay, caught between fire and sea, needed more than food. They needed ships!

Now, providentially it seems, the twenty Greek transport ships that had carried the Greek soldiers away to safety were anchored at Mytilene. So, Asa Jennings lost no time in getting to Mytilene. Surely the Greek ships there would be willing to return to Smyrna and save the Greek people. But General Frankos, in charge of the transports, was cautious and couldn't make up his mind.

It was then that Asa sighted the old USS *Mississippi* at anchor and rowed out through the early morning mist to board her. He was determined to go over the head of General Frankos and make direct contact with the Greek government in Athens.

He told his story to the captain. He then asked that a coded message be sent to Athens requesting that all ships in the waters about Smyrna be placed at his disposal. It was four o'clock in the morning.

A message came back from Athens, "Who are you?"

A natural question. Asa Jennings had been in that part of the world only about a month, and no one had ever heard of him.

He sent back word, "I am in charge of American relief at Mytilene." He didn't explain that he was in charge only by virtue of being the only American there!

Athens outdid General Frankos in caution. The cabinet would have to decide, and the cabinet was not in session. It would meet the next day. What protection would be given the Greek transports? Would American destroyers accompany them? Did that mean that American destroyers would protect the ships if the Turks should try to take them? And so it went.

Finally, at four in the afternoon, the young American's patience was exhausted. He wired Athens that if he did not receive a favorable reply by six o'clock, he would wire openly, without code, letting the whole world know that the Greek government had refused to rescue its own people from certain death.

It worked. Shortly before six o'clock a message came through: ALL SHIPS IN AEGEAN PLACED YOUR COMMAND. REMOVE REFUGEES SMYRNA.

Those ten words meant life for thousands. They also meant that a young, unknown American had just been made admiral of the Greek navy!

And so Asa Jennings assumed command. The captains of the twenty transports were ordered to be ready to leave for Smyrna by midnight. And at that hour they were all in place. Asa Jennings, aboard the lead ship, ordered the Greek flag run down and an American flag flown in its place, with a signal that meant "Follow me." He mounted the bridge and ordered full steam ahead.

Picture the scene if you can. As the ships moved toward Smyrna, Asa could see from his station on the bridge the smoking ruins of what had once been the business section of the city. Directly in front, gaunt brick and stone skeletons of once-beautiful buildings pushed themselves up from the charred debris. And at the water's edge, stretching for miles, was what looked like a lifeless black border. Yet Asa knew that it was a border of living sufferers waiting, hoping, praying—as they had done every moment for days—for ships, ships, ships!

As the transports moved closer and the shore spread out before him, it seemed that every face on that quay was turned toward them and every arm outstretched to bring them in closer. It seemed that the whole shore moved out to grasp them. The air was filled with the cries of those thousands—cries of such joy that the sound pierced to the very marrow of his bones. No need for anyone to tell them what those ships were for. They who had scanned that watery horizon for days, looking wistfully for ships, did not have to be told that here was help, that here was life and safety!

Never had Asa Jennings been so thankful, so truly happy, as on that early morning when he realized that at last—and thank God in time—he had been able to bring hope and a new life to those despairing thousands.

It was Asa Jennings's son who told me this story.

I can never forget it. Nor can I forget the striking parallel that I know will happen soon. A spectacular rescue—not from the sea but from the sky. Involving not three hundred thousand refugees on a single shore but—if only they would be willing—every man, woman, and child on a shaking, burning, convulsing planet. Soon the Savior will descend the flaming skies, accompanied by every angel of heaven, to rescue His faithful people. " 'I will come again,' " He has promised, " 'and receive you to Myself; that where I am, there you may be also' " (John 14:3).

*U*nsettling the Skeptic

One of the most fascinating incidents coming from the annals of a past generation tells of the remarkable conversion of two great men who were avowed skeptics. One was the eminent Gilbert West; the other, Lord Lyttelton, the famous English jurist.

These two men agreed that Christianity should be destroyed. But they also agreed that in order to destroy it, two things were necessary. They must disprove the resurrection of Jesus, and they must discredit the conversion of the apostle Paul.

They divided the task between them. West would assume responsibility for the resurrection, and Lyttelton would care for Paul's experience on the Damascus road. They would give themselves plenty of time—a year or more if necessary. But when they met again to compare notes, each found that the other had become a strong and devoted Christian! Each testified that a remarkable change had occurred in his life through contact with the risen Christ.

I have discovered that if anything will unsettle the skeptic, it likely will not be argument, however sane or sound. Rather, it will be the degree of personal conviction. And that conviction depends entirely upon the reality of one's own commitment to the risen Lord.

A Never-Ending Love Story

Ivory-colored stone, intricately carved and perfectly proportioned, lifts dome and tower above India's plain of Agra. Here, shimmering in the sun beside the Jumna River is the most celebrated building in the world, the Taj Mahal. Many have traveled there to admire its architectural beauty, but few know the equally beautiful story behind it. This magnificent work of art is really about an unusual relationship, the relationship between a Mogul emperor, Shah Jahan, and his beloved wife, Mumtaz Mahal. In a time when royal marriages were almost always a matter of political alliance, these two people united their lives because of love.

At a certain royal bazaar, Jahan fell in love with the woman who is entombed in the Taj Mahal. He asked for her hand in marriage and was accepted. But then he had to wait five long years before court astrologers decreed that the stars were properly aligned for a royal wedding. During that time, Jahan and Mumtaz never met, never saw each other, but their love remained strong. After the wedding, the two became inseparable. Royal poets wrote that the beauty of Mumtaz made the moon hide its face in shame. But Jahan appreciated much more than her physical beauty. His bride proved so intelligent that she soon became his most trusted political advisor. She was generous and compassionate, each day drawing up lists of helpless widows and orphans and making sure their needs were attended to.

Mumtaz bore her husband many children, and despite the complex problems of ruling an empire, Shah Jahan enjoyed an idyllic existence with his wife. When the Shah had to go on a military expedition against rebel forces in the south of India, his queen insisted on going along to be at his side, even though she was pregnant.

It was during this campaign that tragedy struck. After giving birth to her fourteenth child, Mumtaz died. Shah Jahan was devastated. He locked himself in his quarters and refused to eat. He lay moaning on his bed for eight long days, and when he finally emerged, he seemed to have aged several years.

The love of his life was gone. The love that seemed eternal—snatched away. But this man found a way to immortalize his passion. He decided to build a mausoleum for his wife as beautiful as their love.

And so the Taj Mahal was built, an exquisite monument enshrining his wife's remains. The perfect match had been cut short, but Shah Jahan made sure it would be remembered for ages to come in this exquisite structure.

He built a monument to eternal love. When people today stand before this structure, they are really looking at the ideal of undying love, a commitment that transcends even death. And many are moved by the eloquence of this one man's devotion to his wife.

Shah Jahan, the builder of that splendid tomb, experienced one more great tragedy some time after the death of his beloved wife. His own son became greedy for power and turned against him. In 1658 the son led a plot against his father and usurped the throne. Shah Jahan was confined to his own palace. He lived there the last eight years of his life, a prisoner in a gilded cage. But he had one consolation. Through his window he could look out across the Jumna River and see his wife's resting place. The monument still stood, the symbol of his love remained as beautiful as ever.

The Taj Mahal is a wonderful monument to a love that would never die. But, you know, there is a love even stronger and more eternal than the love that is immortalized in this lovely, world-famous building. Our heavenly Father, the King of the universe, says to you and me, " 'I have loved you with an everlasting love; / Therefore with lovingkindness I have drawn you' " (Jeremiah 31:3). And we have this promise from God Himself: " 'I will never leave you nor forsake you' " (Hebrews 13:5).

Freedom From Blindness

In 1929 Frank Morris boarded a ship bound for Switzerland. He had looked forward to the voyage for some time. But a steward was put in charge of his care and kept a very careful eye on the young man. Every night Frank was locked inside his cabin until breakfast! After a quick meal, it was back to his quarters. At ten, Frank could exercise a bit but felt foolish being led around the deck, trotting methodically like a horse. Then the steward deposited Frank in a steamer chair. He met friendly passengers who invited him for a stroll, but the steward always rushed up and objected, saying, "He has to stay where I can keep an eye on him." Every evening at nine the steward tracked Frank down and took him in tow back to the cabin, where he could be locked in for the night.

Frank was an adult, with the normal curiosities and desires of an adult. But he also was blind. The steward assumed he couldn't take care of himself. Frank was treated like an American Express parcel that had to be lugged around. He was a prisoner inside his wall of darkness.

But in Switzerland, Frank made a wonderful discovery—dogs there had been specially trained to guide the blind. He brought one—a German shepherd named Buddy—back to the United States and began an organization called Seeing Eye.

With Buddy at his side, Frank could go almost anywhere, anytime. He demonstrated this ability to a group of reporters at a busy cross street in New York City. Frank and Buddy faced a steady stream of cars and trucks rushing past, blowing horns, screeching brakes. Buddy stepped forward, and Frank followed; he had learned to trust his dog completely. Buddy maneuvered from one lane to another as the cars whizzed past, occasionally stopping, backing up, inching forward. It took three minutes for them to reach the other side of the intersection, but Frank and Buddy made it across safe and sound. The reporters, however, had a more difficult time. Most were still on the other side trying to slip through the traffic. One actually took a cab to get across!

Now Frank knew he was free. He could control his own life. On later voyages across the Atlantic, Frank Morris wandered all over the ship, at all hours, and made many friends. To a man who remembered being dumped at the barbershop every month and waiting there for hours like unclaimed baggage, it was an exciting liberation.

Frank became a free man by learning to depend on Buddy. By trusting his guide completely, he was able to do things even sighted men could not do.

Most of us are not physically blind, but a lot of us have experienced spiritual blindness. We lack the direction, the character qualities, the energy to gain control of our spiritual lives. But God has given us the perfect Counselor for our handicap. The Holy Spirit is the perfect Guide. He longs for us to walk in step with Him.

A Monopoly on the Spirit?

A group of ministers was discussing whether they ought to invite the evangelist Dwight L. Moody to come to their city. He had been quite successful. But one clergyman was unimpressed. He asked, "Does Mr. Moody have a monopoly on the Holy Spirit?"

"No," a colleague replied, "but the Holy Spirit has a monopoly on Mr. Moody!"

Out of the Blue

A young opera student in Munich was practicing a role one day in the garden of his boarding house. He was singing the lines, "Come to me, my love, on the wings of light." Just then, to his utter amazement, a young lady dropped out of the sky and landed at his feet!

His heavenly visitor turned out to be a Bavarian actress who was doing a stunt for a movie. She had parachuted from a plane right into his arms. Love did indeed come to the young student. In a few months the two were married.

That certainly was a remarkable encounter. Most of us realize that spouses don't normally drop out of the sky into our arms. But how many times have we looked for God's will in a particular matter and expected Him to drop an answer or a blessing or a sign down from heaven into our arms? He just might—but we shouldn't expect that this is the usual way He works. He will lead us, but He asks us to listen to His voice in His Word and follow.

Let the Mule Decide?

One day while traveling by mule through the countryside of Spain, Ignatius of Loyola met a follower of Islam, a Moor. The two rode together for a while and struck up a conversation.

The Moor learned that Ignatius was on his way to the Church of Our Lady of Montserrat to do penance. Penance before the virgin Mary. The Moor scoffed at the idea. Ignatius quickly rebuked this "infidel" for his disrespect. The two argued back and forth. Their exchanges grew more heated until the Moor spurred his mount and galloped on ahead.

Ignatius was still furious. He was tempted to hurry after the Moor and kill him. The man had told him where he would leave the highway and follow a trail to a certain village. As Ignatius reached this fork in the road, he couldn't decide what to do. Finally he decided to let his mule be a sign. He dropped the reins on its neck. If the animal followed the Moor's trail, he would kill him. If it stayed on the road, he would let the man live. Fortunately, the mule kept to the easier highway.

In his struggle to decide, Ignatius forgot about God's moral will. God has been very clear that killing is wrong. Jesus has been very clear that we must not hate our neighbor. But instead of sticking to God's clear moral will, Ignatius let his mule decide.

It's dangerous to seek signs or to follow impressions that lead us to go against God's expressed will. It's dangerous to let the mule choose our path.

The Day the Clock Stopped

It was the grand century of knights and queens—Queen Elizabeth and her favorite escort, the Earl of Leicester. The year: 1575.

It was Lord Leicester's desire that the queen visit his proud Kenilworth Castle in the Midlands of the British Isles. She accepted the invitation. Extravagant plans for the celebration were laid. The gardens were exotically trimmed and the castle elegantly decorated. Titled guests were to overflow its courts. Lord Leicester had lavished a fortune on pageantry that excited the entire countryside. Eleven-year-old William Shakespeare might well have trudged the thirteen miles from neighboring Stratford-on-Avon to mingle with the curious spectators.

But on the eve of the visit, Lord Leicester called his servants together for one final word of instruction. "On the morrow," he said, "when the queen steps across the threshold, I ask that the great clock be stopped, never to be started again!"

The morning dawned bright and clear. At the appointed hour the queen's courtiers appeared, the drawbridge was lowered, trumpets blew loud and long. And then, as the queen of England stepped across the threshold into the castle, the great timepiece was stopped, forever marking the historic moment of the queen's arrival.

Talking about clocks—stopped clocks. Time for this aging planet is running out. However graphic the story of Queen Elizabeth's visit to Kenilworth Castle, it is but an inadequate illustration of an hour soon to strike when another Monarch will step across the threshold—this time the threshold of a world.

At that hour, every clock, every watch, every timepiece the world around will be forever stopped, never to be started again. For at that moment, time will be no more. At that moment, when the Savior of our world steps across its threshold as King of kings and Lord of lords, time will melt into eternity.

Safe Only on Your Knees!

A young stranger to the Alps was making his first climb, accompanied by two stalwart guides. It was a steep, hazardous ascent. But he felt secure with one guide ahead and one following. For hours they climbed. And at last, breathless, they reached for those rocks protruding through the snow above them—the summit.

The guide ahead wished to let the stranger have the first glorious view of heaven and earth from the summit and moved aside to let him pass. Forgetting the gales that blew across those summit rocks, the young man leaped to his feet to cross the final distance to the very top of the mountain. But the chief guide dragged him down. "To your knees, sir!" he shouted. "You are never safe here except on your knees!"

Yes, friend, to your knees! No other position is safe in this hour. The summit rocks are just ahead. We hear the roaring of the gales. It is the hour for prayer.

The King Is Coming!

I watched in England with the coronation crowds. All London was a spectacle of fantastic preparation, for royal splendor defies description. As early as twenty-four hours before the dawn of Coronation Day, eager thousands began their struggle for a vantage point along the streets where the procession was to pass. Through the long night they waited patiently. What mattered the cold or the hardness of the sidewalks or the light rain that fell? Were they not to see their queen?

Then as the morning came, those early watchers were joined by multitudes of others banked tier upon tier. Big Ben ticked above them as they watched. Occasionally their patriotic chatter was interrupted by the murmur, "She's coming!" But always there was disappointment.

Big Ben had struck high noon before the coronation was completed at Westminster Abbey. Finally, in the distance the trumpets could be heard, and the waiting throngs—moved with justifiable pride, their eyes filled with tears of joy—passed the cry from mouth to mouth, "The queen is coming! The queen is coming!" I shall never forget how that vast mass of humanity rocked with enthusiasm as at last their newly crowned sovereign appeared. Elizabeth II was queen!

Down along the centuries has echoed the promise of the Savior, "I will come again!" Hardly had He disappeared into the skies when His followers began to look for His return. But always there has been disappointment. God's clock has not yet struck the hour.

Still, one day the hands of God's great timepiece will reach their appointed positions. Someday soon we will hear the sound of the trumpets and the cry will go forth, "The King is coming! The King is coming!" And we shall see Him advancing down the avenue of the heavens accompanied by a glorious retinue of shining angels! Oh, what a day! The long wait will be over, and it will have been well worth every slowly passing minute.

The Last Day on Earth

Vesuvius, almost forgotten, stood close by the city of Pompeii, her rugged slopes covered with vineyards. Scarcely anyone looked her way, and when they did, it was without a trace of apprehension.

The morning dawned like any other summer day in this resort town for wealthy Romans. Little did anyone dream that the sleeping giant five miles away was about to blow her top. True, she had given warnings, but no one seemed to notice.

It was lunchtime. Shopkeepers closed their doors for the long Latin lunch hour. A baker shoved eighty-one loaves of bread into his oven. A customer laid his money on a counter in a wine shop. Then the earthquake came, as if Vesuvius were shaking each inhabitant to rouse him from sleep.

Most of the twenty thousand residents of Pompeii fled. And kept on fleeing. These were the wise. But some lingered—about two thousand—for reasons that today we can read in the ruins of that unfortunate city.

The form of one man was found lying in the street still clutching a handful of gold coins. Some delayed to bury valuables. Others spent precious moments loading carts with their possessions—only to be caught within the circle of death that Vesuvius was inscribing about herself.

Vesuvius was awake now—smoking, rumbling, shaking, and belching forth a river of liquid fire. Rain and ashes were falling over the city. Those who fled through the fields tied pillows over their heads to protect them from falling rock that Vesuvius sent hurtling through the skies.

Lingering inhabitants breathed deadly sulfur fumes and dropped in their tracks, where they were encased with a mixture of rain and ashes like a plaster cast. Encased in this way, there can be seen today the very forms of those who waited too long.

Entire families were caught in the trap of death, the terror on their faces preserved to this day. There is evidence that even after they fell, some tried to rise again. But death was in the air.

Life in Pompeii had stopped with the awesome hush of death. The shops were never opened after that lunch hour. The barmaid never picked up the customer's money. The eighty-one loaves of bread were never taken from the oven. And those foolish carts, loaded with unimportant possessions, still blocked the narrow passageways.

August 24, A.D. 79 was a deadline written in ashes. The bricks and stones cry out. They tell us the tragic story of the last night of Pompeii.

I have thought a lot about that last night in Pompeii. God pleads most urgently with the human heart just before it is forever cut off. No doubt many could not sleep that last night. From all the evidence, one after another gave himself over to a night of abandon in order to escape the voice of the Spirit.

But, thank God, friend, for that voice! It is our only hope—the voice of conscience, the voice of conviction. How else can God speak to the human heart? How else can He warn us of impending danger?

*L*ittle Acts of Kindness

Madge was busily preparing to fly home to be with her mother. Several members of their family had been killed in a car crash. The terrible news came just as Madge, her husband, and children were preparing to move to a new state. The house was in chaos. Somehow Madge had to get ready for the funeral. She had to find the right clothes for everyone in all the boxes and suitcases. As she was walking around the house in a daze, aimlessly picking up things and putting them down, the doorbell rang. It was a neighbor.

"I've come to clean your shoes," he said.

Madge didn't understand. So the neighbor explained, "When my father died, it took me hours to get the children's shoes cleaned and shined for the funeral. So, that's what I've come to do for you."

The neighbor settled himself on the kitchen floor and scraped and washed and shined all the shoes in the house. Watching him concentrate quietly on his task helped Madge pull her thoughts together and begin her preparations. Later, when Madge returned from the laundry room, the neighbor was gone. But lined neatly against the wall stood all their shoes, spotless and gleaming.

Little acts of kindness can make such a difference!

*D*on't Stop for Anything!

It was June 14, 1975. Murray Hughes, eight years old, and his sister Roslyn, six, were in the back seats of the plane—their shoes off and the seatbelts tight—when it crashed in a remote section of the Australian outback. They were not hurt. But their father slumped unconscious in the pilot seat, and their mother was pinned in the cockpit.

Murray couldn't forget the desperation in his mother's voice as she cried, "Take Rossie and go get help! Don't stop for anything!"

The children couldn't find their shoes, so they started out without them. And for twelve hours they stumbled barefoot down the snake-infested mountainside, thinking only of their broken and bleeding parents up there in the fog-enshrouded forest.

Again and again they prayed, "Please, God, make us brave."

A rancher spotted them in a pasture seven miles from the wreckage. He said, "They were just babies. I couldn't believe it when I saw them out there." They were shivering from the cold, their clothes in tatters. They were badly scratched, and their feet were bleeding.

"The little girl was very brave," said the rancher, "clutching a small purse with a brush and comb inside. The boy came up and told me to get help for his mother and father. He was the bravest boy I'd ever come across. His feet were cut up real bad, but he didn't want to rest. He had just one thought in mind—to get help for his parents."

The organizer of the rescue party said, "You may think twelve hours isn't a long time. But this is some of the toughest country there is. It's dense forest, and the bush is alive with deadly snakes and poisonous spiders. I don't think those two kids could have survived much longer out there."

Roslyn told about their ordeal. She said, "Mommy told us to be brave and go for help. It was very misty, and we couldn't see where we were going. The trees had big roots sticking out of the ground, and I kept tripping over them.

"The ground was very rough," she went on. "Mommy told us to take our shoes off in the plane so that we would be more comfortable, and when the crash happened, we couldn't find them. It hurt when we walked on the ground. There were rough stones, and I kept stubbing my toes.

"We were very scared. We kept hearing rustling noises all around us. Once there was a very loud rustling in the bushes right next to us. I screamed. Murray was very brave. He put his arm around me and said, 'Don't worry. I won't let anything hurt you.' "

Murray said, "I was very scared, but I didn't want Rossie to know. I just kept thinking about Mommy and Daddy and how we had to get help. I have never walked so far. The worst part was having no shoes. . . . Every now and then Rossie would stop and cry. Sometimes I would let her lie down for a while."

The rescue party was too late. And Murray wept. "I only wish we could tell Mommy and Daddy that we tried our best."

How like what Jesus did! People He had made, on a planet He had created, were in trouble. Without help they couldn't survive. And He said, "I'll go, Father." And the Father said, "Go, Son. And don't stop for anything!"

He left His crown behind. It would have been easier with His crown— so much easier. But He didn't stop for anything. All He could think of was finding help—finding a way to save you and me.

A Recipe for Happiness

There was a couple who was about to celebrate their golden wedding anniversary. The local newspaper sent out a reporter for an interview, and only the husband was at home.

"What is your recipe for a long, happy marriage?" asked the reporter.

"Well, I'll tell you, young fellow," the old gentleman said slowly. "I was an orphan, and I always had to work pretty hard for my board and keep. I never even looked at a girl until I was grown. Sarah was the first one I ever kept company with. When she maneuvered me into proposing, I was scared stiff. But after the wedding, her pa took me aside and handed me a little package. 'Here is all you really need to know,' he said. And this is what was in the package."

He reached for a large gold watch in his pocket, opened it, and handed it to the reporter. There across the face of the watch, where he could see it a dozen times a day, were written these words: *Say something nice to Sarah.*

The Remarkable Story of Harold Hughes

Harold remembered the men overseas that he had shot and realized he would make a terrible mess in the bedroom. So, carefully holding a Remington twelve-gauge shotgun, he walked down the hall and into the bathroom. He was trying desperately to escape his broken promises, his web of lies, trying to escape the hurt in his children's eyes. He had decided that this was the only way out of the bottle. Harold stepped into the bathtub, lay down, and pointed the shotgun's muzzle into his mouth.

When Harold Hughes first took a drink, he was a shy, tongue-tied teenager. The fiery sting of alcohol burned his throat, and yet it made him feel like he was walking on air. Suddenly he could talk to girls. He was confident, relaxed, the life of the party.

Harold also found that he wanted three drinks for every one his buddies ordered. Something inside urged him on and on. His mother often told him, "Harold, I believe God has something special for you. You must keep yourself fit for it." Her son made promises but couldn't stop going out with the guys.

Harold received a scholarship to study aeronautical engineering at the University of Iowa. After only a year, he dropped out and married petite, raven-haired Eva. They were happy—when Harold wasn't drinking.

Then Harold's brother, Jesse, died in a car accident, and Harold drank more—to forget. During World War II, Harold served as an infantryman in bloody campaigns in North Africa and Italy. He had even more to forget when he returned home to Eva and his two small daughters.

Harold became a partner in a trucking business and did well. But his work often kept him out late, out late drinking with business associates. When Eva tried to talk to him about his drinking, Harold became angry and belligerent. When sober, he noticed the dark circles under his wife's eyes. His girls sometimes hid in the closet when he came home. Finally, Eva and the girls left the house. Harold was moved to make a solemn promise. He swore before a judge that he would not touch liquor for one year.

A few weeks later, Harold traveled to a truckers' meeting in Ames, Iowa. One morning he woke up in a hotel in Des Moines. He had no idea how he had gotten there. A neon sign flashed outside his window. A familiar dry, stale taste lingered in his mouth. As he stood up, the room spun. Staggering into the bathroom to wash his face, he noticed vomit splattered on the toilet.

One more promise down the drain. After Des Moines, Harold made no more pretense about trying to stop. He came home drunk more and more often. Then on one fateful day in 1952, Harold promised Eva he would be home early for an important dinner date. But after a business meeting he lingered for "just one more drink." Before he knew it, it was 11:00 P.M. Harold hurried home, but Eva and the girls were gone.

That night, sitting in an empty house, his repeated failures overwhelmed him. For ten years alcohol had dominated his life. He made promises, he prayed, but nothing could control his craving. Harold had failed everyone who meant anything to him. A terrible self-hatred nauseated him.

What was the point of living? There was only one way to end the hell his family had to endure. Eva was still young and pretty; she would marry again. His girls would be able to forget him, and they would be spared the disgrace of having a drunk for a father.

Harold slid three shells into the Remington and pumped one into the chamber. The porcelain of the bathtub felt cold as he lay down. He reached down with his thumb for the trigger.

Harold Hughes felt this was the only solution to a problem he had tried desperately to overcome. He felt himself a prisoner to alcohol. There in the bathtub, about to pull the trigger, Harold was struck with a thought—suicide is wrong in God's eyes. And yet, his whole life seemed wrong. In a few years his family would get over his death and have a chance to rebuild their lives. But if he remained, he would never change and would hurt them even more.

Harold thought he should explain all this to God before pulling the trigger. So, he climbed out of the bathtub and knelt on the cold, hard floor. "Oh, God," Harold groaned, "I'm a failure, a drunk, a liar. . . . I'm lost and hopeless and want to die. Forgive me for doing this." Harold broke into sobs. "Oh, Father," he continued, "please take care of Eva and the girls. Please help them forget me."

Then he slipped to the floor, shaking with heavy sobs, and cried out to God until he lay still, exhausted. Harold then began to feel a peace he had never felt before. It seemed to drive out all his emptiness, self-hatred, and condemnation. He felt a strange joy welling up inside.

He rose to his knees and gave himself totally to God. "Whatever You ask me to do, Father," he said. "I will do it."

Harold felt that he had met a living God who reached down to him, Someone who cared and comforted him. He began a regular program of prayer and Bible study. He made a commitment to stay away from alcohol altogether. Harold Hughes had begun the road to recovery. It wouldn't be easy; there would be struggles. But he knew God would give him the spiritual strength to persevere.

Harold's story has a remarkable ending. The despairing alcoholic went on to become the governor of Iowa and later a distinguished member of the United States Senate. But one event stands out in his mind as a symbol of his transformation. More important to him than all the public honors he later earned was one small incident that occurred shortly after his commitment to Christ.

Harold was studying the Bible alone in his living room one evening when he felt a nudge at his elbow. He looked up. It was Connie and Carol, his two small daughters, standing quietly in their nightgowns. They had changed so much—and he had missed so much.

Then Carol, the youngest, said, "Daddy, we've come to kiss you good night."

The father's eyes blurred. It had been so long since the children had come to his embrace. Now their beautiful, clear eyes held no fear. Daddy had come home at last.

$\mathcal{I}$f you enjoyed this book, you'll want to read these also.

Planet Still in Rebellion

George E. Vandeman. Today events seem to be spiraling out of control as never before. The evening news often presents a picture of a confused world filled with mindless violence. Is there any way to make sense of the bewildering chaos? Today, as never before, we need a sure word. We need the promise of the Bible—"Man shall not live by bread alone, but by every word that proceedeth out of the mouth of God" (Matthew 4:4).

ISBN 13: 978-0-8163-2131-5.   ISBN 10: 0-8163-2131-0.
Paperback, 128 pages.

Also available:

Planet Still in Rebellion—Audio book 4CDs
Read by Fred Kinsey. UPC: 4333003767.
Produced by Connie Vandeman Jeffery
Adventist Media Center

NEW!
The Invitation

Alejandro Bullón. Evangelist Alejandro Bullón shares breathtaking stories of people destroyed by life's circumstances and rebuilt by the love of God. You may think that your life makes no sense, that there is no forgiveness or hope for you. Yet, each of these stories will lead you to believe in a Power that is above and beyond your own self. The great need of every man and woman is God's great opportunity to save you. He offers you a new birth, a new life with meaning, the opportunity to rebuild your life and restore your family. Please, accept His invitation. A great sharing book!

ISBN 13: 978-0-8163-2252-7.   ISBN 10: 0-8163-2252-X.
Paperback, 144 pages.

Three Ways to Order:
1. Local Adventist Book Center®
2. Call 1-800-765-6955
3. Shop AdventistBookCenter.com